DELEGATE FROM
NEW JERSEY

Monday April 5th 1779 Commercial Committee
Congress. A Number of Letters Read.
Clothier Generals Pay, the Report was 1000 D[ollars] 12 Ration
and forrege for 3 Horses long debate, cari for 15000
States Clothier to be appointed & Paid by the State
Commissary Turnbulls affair came on but not
finish.

Tuesday April 6th. Commercial Committee
Congress. Mr Rutgers and Mr Horton appointed Deputy
Muster Masters. Mr McPherson nominated
Order of the Day. Long Debate about Mr Dean and the
Commissioners abroad, on the Report of the Committee
on foreign Affairs.
P.M. Marine Committee.

Wednesday April 7th 1779 Commercial Committee.
Congress. Sundry Letters Read. Motion for 15000 L[ivres]
to be Paid to Captains, McNutt, Nevers, & Rogers, they
are to endeavor to open a Road in to Nova Scotia.
Order of the day, for examening in to the conduct of the
Commissioners abroad, and foreign Affairs, great and
warm debates. agreed to Read all the Letters.

DELEGATE FROM NEW JERSEY

The Journal of John Fell

Edited with an Introduction by
Donald W. Whisenhunt

National University Publications
KENNIKAT PRESS • 1973
Port Washington, N.Y. • London

Copyright © 1973 by Donald W. Whisenhunt. All Rights Reserved. No part of this publication may be reproduced, stored in a retrieval system, or transmitted, in any form or by any means, electronic, mechanical, photocopying, recording, or otherwise, without the prior written permission of the publisher.

Library of Congress Catalog Card No.: 73-83264
ISBN: 0-8046-9041-3

Manufactured in the United States of America

Published by
Kennikat Press, Inc.
Port Washington, N.Y./London

To
Donald and Ben

Two of the many
for whom John Fell labored

PREFACE

As we approach the American Revolution Bicentennial, our thoughts turn to proper and fitting commemorations. Certainly, one way is to revive the memories of the unsung, but vital, actors in the drama. John Fell must undoubtedly fall into this category.

Fell's diary, covering the first year of his service in the Continental Congress, from November 6, 1778, to November 30, 1779, has remained unnoticed for many years in the Library of Congress.

For help in rescuing it from obscurity several notes of appreciation are in order. A modest grant from the New Jersey Historical Commission made possible my first work on the document. The staff of the Manuscripts Division of the Library of Congress is to be thanked for assisting me in every way to reproduce the diary as close to its original form as possible. I am likewise appreciative of the encouragement that has come from my Academic Dean, Dr. Richard W. Solberg. The student assistant of the History Department at Thiel College, Thomas Scabareti, was very helpful in proofreading. Above all,

Delegate from New Jersey

I thank my wife for allowing John Fell to become a part of our household for two years.

          Donald W. Whisenhunt

Greenville, Pa.
November 1, 1972

CONTENTS

INTRODUCTION	3
BIOGRAPHY OF JOHN FELL	6
JOURNAL OF JOHN FELL	13
BRIEF BIOGRAPHIES	152
BIBLIOGRAPHICAL NOTE	204
INDEX	206

DELEGATE FROM
NEW JERSEY

1775	Emissions	Bro't Over
June 22.	2,000,000	1779 February 3. 5000,160
July 25.	1,000,000	19. 5,000,160
Nov'r 29.	3,000,000	Ap'l 1. 5000,160
1776 June 5.	10,000 to be &c.	
Feb'y	4,000,000	
May	Sam Wilkinson	
9.	5,000,000	
July 22	5,000,000	
Nov 2	500,000	
Dec'r 28	5,000,000	
1777 Feb'y 26	5,000,000	
May 20	5,000,000	
Aug 15	1,000,000	
Nov'r 7	1,000,000	
Dec'r 3	1,000,000	
1778 Jan'y 8	1,000,000	
22	2,000,000	
Feb'y 16	2,000,000	
Mar 5	2,000,000	
Ap'l 4	1,000,000	
11	5,000,000	
18	500,000	
May 22	5,000,000	
June 20	5,000,000	
July 30	5,000,000	
Sep'r 5	5,000,000	
26	10,000,100	
Nov 4	10,000,100	
Dec'r 14	10,000,100	
	102,000,300	

Journal
Kept by Judge
John Fell —
while Member
of
Congress
for
The State of New Jersey
1778.

INTRODUCTION

SINCE THIS IS the printing of a document written almost two hundred years ago, several comments are necessary about the format and style that have been used.

It has been the desire of the editor to reproduce Fell's diary as close to the original form as possible. However, due to printing difficulties and the concern for readability, a few changes have been made.

The diary entries are reproduced in chronological order. The annotations or notes of explanation about the immediately preceding diary entry are printed in a distinctive style. When the diary is clear as to meaning, no notes have been added. The editor has endeavored to keep the notes as brief as possible; however, there are places where an explanation is needed.

The diary entries are exactly as Fell wrote them, with the following exceptions. The dates have all been standardized for readability and convenience in using the book. On a few Sundays, Fell entered the date in the diary but made no comment. Such entries have been deleted. Fell used abbreviations and contractions extensively, and, in the fashion of the day, parts of the abbreviated or contracted words were written in superscript above the regular line. In this edition, his abbreviations have been retained, but for consistency and readability they have been printed on the same line in the same type size. The editor has not utilized apostrophes with abbreviations because Fell used the apostrophe extensively and often in unusual places. To have added apostrophes would have led to confusion and unnecessary cluttering of the text.

Bracketed matter in diary entries was inserted by the editor and consists mostly of the correct spelling of names. Although a few names are repeated, the editor believes this is necessary for easier identification and for ease in consulting the editor's biographical sketches. Every attempt was made to check the spellings of names, but in a few instances when it was impossible to substantiate Fell, no bracketed insertions have been made. Occasionally, bracketed marks of punctuation have been included for clarity and readability. In a few instances, editorial comments are also included within brackets.

Fell regularly used graphic symbols or abbreviations, but since these are fairly common no explanation is given in the text. He often used &c., another form of etc., and N.B., the abbreviation of the Latin phrase *nota bene* or note well. He also used Do and do (ditto) extensively. In such cases the editor has placed in brackets the words he was repeating in this fashion.

Very few liberties have been taken with the text of Fell's diary. This document reflects the personality of the man, and too much editing would destroy that. The desire has been to allow Fell to speak for himself; if that has been achieved the effort will have been worthwhile.

In the latter portion of the book are biographical

Introduction

sketches of those mentioned in the diary. The sketches are not meant to be complete biographies but to give enough information so that the reader will know something about each person. The editor especially emphasized the role or importance of the individual mentioned at the time that the diary was kept. For some fifty out of the two hundred fifty names mentioned by Fell nothing could be found in the standard reference or biographical works, and no further attempt was made to identify the person; in the very brief sketches, nothing more could be learned about the persons than is provided.

BIOGRAPHY of JOHN FELL

JOHN FELL was one of those obscure men who is often overlooked in the larger picture of American history. He was no firebrand like Patrick Henry, no man with words like Thomas Jefferson, no military genius like George Washington. Instead he was one of those men who fulfills his duties every day in a routine and unnoticed manner. He was a citizen of the highest virtue, deeply committed to the goal of Independence. Truly an unsung hero of the Revolutionary period, he was firm in his conviction, true to his ideals, loyal to his friends, totally dependable, and unquestionable in integrity. It is very accurate to say that "few men have been so solidly useful and so obscure."[1]

Very little is known about Fell's early life. He was apparently born and educated in New York City. He was a descendant of one Symon Fell, who is recorded as aiding in the defense of the city in 1655 while it was still a Dutch colony.[2] He was married to Susanna Marschalk, or Moskhk, widow of a Mr. McIntosh. They had one son, Peter Renaudet,[3] and a daughter, Elizabeth, who later married the grandson of the Lieutenant Governor of New York, Cadwallader Colden.[4]

By 1759 he was the senior partner in the firm of John Fell & Company in New York. He was obviously a man of some means, since his firm had several armed merchant vessels on the sea by 1759. His style of life in New York and later in New Jersey and in the Continental Congress attests to his wealth and standing. He lived well and was a close friend of many of the most prominent men of the day.[5]

After he had established himself in New York, Fell purchased an estate of 220 acres near Paramus in Bergen County, New Jersey. It is not clear if he gave up his mercantile interests; and the date of his move to New Jersey is unknown. He named his new estate Petersfield. There is some speculation that he was following the custom of that day in naming one's home. Possibly, he was imitating Colonel Philip Schuyler, who had named his estate Peterboro. There is additional speculation that the name was in honor of one of his ancestors, but it is logical to assume that it was named for his son, Peter, who may well have been named for an ancestor.[6]

In the 1760's Fell became active in New Jersey affairs. In 1766 he was made a judge of the Court of Common Pleas and held the position until 1774. He was later named to the same position again from 1776 to 1786. From the beginning of the spread of Revolutionary sentiment throughout the colonies, Fell was found in the forefront of the radical cause. On June 25, 1774, he was a leader of a group of 328 citizens of Bergen County who signed patriotic resolutions at Hackensack Court House pledging themselves to support and aid the resistance to Great Britain.[7]

Fell became the chairman of the Bergen County Committee charged with gaining support and resisting the British locally.[8] In this position, he gained the reputation of being "a great Tory hunter."[9] He was also the chairman of the local standing Committee of Correspondence. In the summer of 1775 he was elected a member of the Provincial Congress meeting at Trenton, and in 1776 he was a member of the Provincial Council in the first state legislature.[10]

Fell's activities in strengthening the Revolutionary hold on Bergen County were apparently successful and serious enough for the British to consider him dangerous. Consequently, on the night of April 22, 1777, he was taken prisoner at his home by twenty-five Loyalist raiders.[11]

Fell was sent to New York, where he was imprisoned in the provost jail on either April 23 or 24.[12] During his confinement, he was mistreated severely by the British. One report indicated that he was denied medicine and the care of a physician when he was extremely ill with a fever.[13] Despite the fact that he was a personal acquaintance of the commander, General Robertson, his treatment did not improve. There is some reason to believe that Robertson did not see him for six months after his arrest and that even then the improved conditions that he promised were not forthcoming.

When word of his ill-treatment reached New Jersey, the State Committee of Safety offered in October 1777 to exchange two of its British prisoners, James Parker and Walter Rutherford, for Fell and another prisoner, Wynant Van Zandt. When this appeal was rejected, the Committee ordered Parker and Rutherford imprisoned in the Morris County jail in retaliation. After about eight months detention, Fell was paroled on January 7, 1778, and on the following May 11 he was released.[14]

Biography of John Fell

On November 6, 1778, Fell was elected a delegate from New Jersey to the Continental Congress, where he served until November 28, 1780, having been re-elected on May 25 and December 25, 1779. After leaving Congress, he served in 1782-1783 on the New Jersey Council. He continued as a judge of the Court of Common Pleas until 1786.[15]

In 1793, in his declining years, he sold his estate in New Jersey to John H. Thompson, a New York merchant, for £2,000. He then took up residence at the home in Coldenham, Duchess County, New York, formerly belonging to his son, who had died in 1789. Fell apparently lived there with his three grandchildren until his death on May 15, 1798.[16]

The diary kept by Fell during his first year of service as a member of the Continental Congress and the other records that mention him show him to be a very firm and decisive man. He was among the most regular and dependable members, at least during his first year of service. He missed only two weekends, when he visited friends near Philadelphia; two weeks, when he returned home for a short visit; and one ten-day period, when he was ill. Apparently, regular attendance was a matter of some pride to him, especially since he faithfully recorded in his diary the absences of his colleagues from New Jersey, Witherspoon, Scudder, Houston, and Frelinghuysen. He may well have made these notes to protect himself against possible charges of neglect of the state's interests. On several occasions New Jersey was not officially represented in Congress since Fell was the only delegate in attendance and the state required that two at least be present. In the matter of attendance Fell surpasses the other New Jersey delegates.

Fell's diary and the *Journals* of the Continental Congress also show him to be a man of firm fiscal responsibility. He was reluctant to support movements to inflate the already weak currency and to increase the nation's indebtedness, which was already so great that some questioned the government's solvency. Despite this concern, he nevertheless voted to do what he considered necessary for a vigorous prosecution of the war.

He emerges from the record as a man very impatient with inefficiency and the waste of time. He was especially distressed by the bickering among members of Congress and the excessive amounts of time devoted to such issues as the Deane-Lee controversy, the Laurens-Morris affair, and the dispute between Benedict Arnold and the state officials of Pennsylvania.

He appears to have been a cautious man who was willing to accept independence without satisfaction of all the demands made by many members of Congress. The insistence by some members on extensive fishing rights off the coast of Newfoundland especially distressed him. Likewise, he was fearful that excessive demands for navigation rights on the Mississippi River might prolong the war to the nation's disadvantage and risk losing everything.

Fell seemed to think that the first order of business was to obtain independence as quickly and as decisively as possible. Afterwards, he believed, we could negotiate from a position of peace and strength to achieve the other things that might rightfully belong to the United States.

During his Congressional career Fell was not an outspoken man. He is recorded as voting 265 times, but he made few motions and wrote fewer reports.[17] His major work was on the Commercial Committee, which he attended almost daily with a near-religious devotion. It was here that he made his contribution in his insistence on fiscal responsibility. In addition, he served on a few special committees and on the Marine and the special committee of 12 on foreign affairs.

Unquestionably, Fell was a valuable citizen during his own lifetime and in the future development of his country. Without innumerable others like him, the course of the Revolutionary movement would have been greatly different. His great misfortune, from the historical viewpoint, was in not being an aggressive or spectacular personality. As a result he was overshadowed by the more dominant people. It seems safe to say that without men like Fell to support and defend them, the careers of the better known figures might have been much different.

Notes

1. Allen Johnson and Dumas Malone (eds.), *Dictionary of American Biography* (20 vols.; New York, 1928-1936), VI, 314.
2. *Ibid.*
3. "Fell, John," *New Jersey Historical Society Collections*, IX (1916), 110-111.
4. William Nelson, New Jersey in the Revolution," *New Jersey Archives*, 2d ser. I (1901), 55n.
5. *Ibid.*
6. *Ibid.*, 54n.
7. Johnson and Malone, *loc. cit.*
8. *Ibid.*
9. "Journals of Stephen Kemble," *New York Historical Society Collections*, (1883), 114.
10. Johnson and Malone, *loc. cit.*

11. *New Jersey Historical Society Collections*, 110.
12. "Journals of Stephen Kemble," 114.
13. *Proceedings of the New Jersey Historical Society,* n.s., V (1920), 177.
14. *New Jersey Historical Society Collections*, 110.
15. Johnson and Malone, *loc. cit.*
16. *New Jersey Historical Society Collections*, 111.
17. Johnson and Malone, *loc. cit.*

THE JOURNAL

Sunday, Nov. 29, 1778

Left Petersfield. Dined at Aquackina, Lay at Newark.

> Petersfield was his estate of 220 acres near Paramus in Bergen County.

Monday, Nov. 30

Dined 5 Mile from Elizabethtown, Lay at Mr Marrinors at Brunswick. (Coll Nelson [John Neilson] told me, he declined going to Congress. [ )]

Tuesday, Dec. 1

Dined at Princeton, Spent the Evening with Governor Levingston [Livingston] at Trenton.

Wednesday, Dec. 2

Dined at Trenton, Received from the Secretary

of New Jersey my Credentials to Congress. Lay at Bristol.

Thursday, Dec. 3

Dined at Frankford, Lay at Philadelphia. (At Mr Whiteheads.[ )]

Friday, Dec. 4

at Do [Whitehead's] Peter R Fell Returned home.

> Peter R. Fell was his son. Apparently, he accompanied his father to Philadelphia.

Saturday, Dec. 5

was Introduced to Congress.

Sunday, Dec. 6

Dined with Mr Isaac Moses

Monday, Dec. 7

Honble John Jay Esqr, took his seat in Congress.

> John Jay was at the same time the Chief Justice of the Supreme Court of New York. By special action, the New York legislature had decided to appoint a member of the court as a delegate to Congress.

Tuesday, Dec. 8

John Temple Esqr, Dined at Mr Whiteheads

> A letter from President M. Weare of New

The Journal

Hampshire concerning John Temple was read and tabled.

Wednesday, Dec. 9

Honble Henry Laurens Esqr Resign'd his Chair as President of Congress

> Laurens resigned because of the controversy concerning Silas Deane's acquisition of supplies from France. Arthur Lee, another American minister, charged that the supplies were meant to be gifts, while Deane argued that they were purchases. This acrimonious debate divided Congress into two hostile camps. Laurens felt that his honor had been questioned and he could no longer serve as president of Congress although he had every intention to remain an active member.

Thursday, Dec. 10

Honble John Jay Esqr was Elected President in the Room of Mr Laurens Resign'd for Mr Jay 8 States, Mr Laurens 4. Virginia not Represented. Dined with Mr Laurens

> There is no recorded vote on this election in the *Journals*. Apparently, not enough Virginia delegates were present to represent that state.

Delegate from New Jersey

Friday, Dec. 11

Coll Scudder gon home, State of New Jersey not Represented.

> This implies that Fell was the only New Jersey delegate present since for representation the state required the vote of at least two of the five delegates.

Saturday, Dec. 12

A Number of Petitions & Memorials A Letter from Genl Washington, was read advising that the Enemy had left the North River &c.

Sunday, Dec. 13

A great deal of Rain, Dined with Mr Levy.

Monday, Dec. 14

Letter from Count Polaska [Pulaski] Read referrd to the Board of Warr.

Tuesday, Dec. 15

Dr Wetherspoon [Witherspoon] came to Congress

> Witherspoon was Fell's colleague from New Jersey. Since he was absent very often, Fell usually records his attendance.

Wednesday, Dec. 16

Motion from one of the Treasury to take out of Circulation all the Emissions of May 20, 1777 and April 1778. 41 Million 500   30 million on Loan and 15 Million by Taxes for the Year 1779. Genl St Clairs acquital confirm'd New Jersey divided   Dr Weatherspoon [Witherspoon] No.

> The total amount to be withdrawn from circulation was $41,500,000. This proposal and the motion to raise the taxes from $10 to $15 million were approved. General St. Clair had been court-martialed in September 1778 for evacuating Fort Ticonderoga in face of the enemy. He was completely exonerated by the tribunal. Congress, in this instance, simply confirmed the acquittal. Fell voted to sustain the decision.

Thursday, Dec. 17

Sieur Gerrard [Gerard], requested to Ship 6000 Casks of Rice, Reccomended to the State of So Carolina to allow it; Letter read from Genl Washington at Middle Brook, Relating to the disappointment of the Commissioners, who went to Amboy to meet the British Commissioners to setle an Exchange of Prisoners, Committee appointed to answer the General, Mr Laurens, Burk [Burke], Smith & Morris, Motion for Purchasing Horses in Virginia, Postponed to consult with the General[.] Motion on fineance for the Bills to be cancelld by the first of June, for Weatherspoon [Witherspoon], Duane, Geary [Gerry], Ellsworth, agst. Smith & Burk [Burke]. Dined with President Jay. Commercial Committee appointed vizt. Mesrs Laurens, Smith, Lewis[,] Searle and Fell.

> The request of Gerard is recorded under December 16 in the *Journals*. In the committee to confer with Washington, Fell omits the name of Samuel Adams. The appointment of the Commercial Committee was actually made on December 14. Why Fell waited to enter it here is not clear. He may simply have forgotten to do so earlier.

Friday, Dec. 18

Letter from General Lee, Requesting the minutes of all the Proceedings relating to him; Do [letter] from Mr Marlbon [Evan Malbone] Rhode Island, requesting to bring his Effects from Jamaica

> General Charles Lee was found guilty in a court-martial of disobedience of orders, misbehavior before the enemy, and disrespect for the Commander-in-Chief during the Battle of Monmouth. His mild punishment was suspension from the army for one year. Following the trial, he often wrote Congress in an insulting manner.

Saturday, Dec. 19

Genl Lee to be furnish'd with all the Proceedings from the Reccords relating to his tryal; Motion to confer with Gl Washington on ways and means to reduce the Expences of the Army, referrd to a Committee of 5. vizt. Laurens, Duane, Geary

The Journal

[Gerry], Ellsworth, & Smith. Dined with General De Portaile [du Portail].

Sunday, Dec. 20

Commercial Committee met at Mr Laurens's agreed to meet to morrow morning at 9. O Clock to choose a Secretary.

Monday, Dec. 21

Commercial Committee 9 oClock. Present, Smith, Lewis[,] Searle & my Self chose Mr Lawrence [Laurens] Chairman & Major Moses Young Secretary. Congress. 11 A M, great debates about calling in the money so soon, ought not to be till money can be ready to be Exchanged for it. Commercial Committee to setle Mr Saml Cursons acct. Mr Root Balloted, for the Board of Warr. This day came to Lodge at the house of Mrs Gibbons in Spruce Street.

> The referral of the Curson affair was actually made on December 18. Root was elected to the Board of War on December 22.

Tuesday, Dec. 22

Memorial Read from Mr Sutton Pay Master for the Loss of Money, carr'd in the negative. At 6 P M, Mr Deane attended Congress

> According to the *Journals,* the memorial from Captain John Sutton was recommitted.

Wednesday, Dec. 23

Mr Deane attending this morning did not go to Committee, Genl Washington visited Congress; At 6 P M Genl Thompson with two witnesses were Examin'd at the Barr. NB Genl Lee & Lt Coll Laurens fought a Duel

> General Washington did not formally attend Congress this day. The record shows that he arrived in town on the night of December 22, so he may well have attended informally. General William Thompson, an American officer on parole by the British, felt that Thomas McKean had hindered his exchange. After attacks on McKean and on Congress, he was judged to be in disrespect of Congress. This decision had been made on November 23, but the case continued to drag on. General Charles Lee became so abusive of Congress and General Washington that Colonel John Laurens, son of Henry Laurens, challenged him to a duel. Lee was wounded so that he was unable to answer another challenge from Anthony Wayne.

Thursday, Dec. 24

A motion for the Secretary to wait on Genl Washington to desire his attendance President told him a Committee would be appointed to consult with him Respecting the ensuing Campaign, he with drew, the Committee Laurens, Duane,

Smith, Root, and Morris: The remainder of the day in debate about Genl Thompson, whether Judge Atleys [Atlee] deposition be admitted, carried in the Negative., Motion whether the General is guilty of a breach of Priviledge agst. the member Honble Mr McKean   Carried in the Afirmitave, my Vote no. then whether the Generals deffence should be allow'd as a full justification, carried in the afirmitive   so ended an unhappy dispute that has given Congress a great deal of trouble between Genl Thompson & the Honble Member for the State of Delaware, to morrow being Christmas Day adjournd to Saturday.

> Fell often was exasperated with the time wasted by Congress on trifling matters. Apparently, he thought General Thompson was innocent and was glad to have the matter settled.

Friday, Dec. 25

This day is excesive Cold with Snow & Ice in the River. has been sevearly Cold for some days past.

Saturday, Dec. 26

Excesive cold morning, Commercial Committee, Present Mr Lawrence [Laurens] agreed to meet Mr Mumford to morrow morning   11 A M Congress, A Letter from Abm Clark was Read, with a complaint agst. Genl Maxwell for refusing to deliver some Prisoners detain by him and de-

Delegate from New Jersey

manded by a Habeus Corpus refferd to a Committee of 3. vizt. Mr Duane, Mr Burk [Burke] & Mr Fell, A Memorial was Read Complaining of sundry abuses of Capt Cunningham of the Revenge. Reffer'd to the Marine Committee. Motion for the Emitions of May 1777 and April 1778 to be brought in by the first June and not afterwards redeemable.

> On December 22 the *Journals* record that a memorial from Mumford was read in Congress.

Sunday, Dec. 27

Commercial Committee 9 oClock am

Monday, Dec. 28

Commercial Committee. do [9 o'clock] 11 A M. Went to Congress, but not being Members sufficient no Congress.

Tuesday, Dec. 29

Commercial Committee 9 oClock. 11 am Congress. This morning waited on General Washington, about the Exchange of Lashier [Loziers] & Brower his answer that he had allready demanded them of Sr [Sir] Henry Clinton. A Request from the French Minister to Prevent the Carrying Masts from New Hampshire and the Masachusets Bay to St. Domingo for fear of falling in to the hands of the Enemy Motion for 2 Brigr Gen-

The Journal

erals for North Carolina 1 for Philadelphia & 1 for So Carolina. Finance

> There is no mention in the *Journals* about Washington's visit. The French minister reported that enemy ships were in great need of masts, and he was afraid of them falling into enemy hands. A committee was appointed to investigate the need of an additional brigadier general in Pennsylvania, not Philadelphia as Fell reports.

Wednesday, Dec. 30

Thanksgiving day, No Congress.

> Fell implies that no Congress was scheduled for this day. The *Journals* report that there was no session because of a lack of a quorum.

Thursday, Dec. 31

did not go to the Commercial Committee   Congress. Mr S Deane attended with his Narative Sundry Letters read from Genl Gates, Genl Phillips &c. finance &c.

> This related to Deane's activities while in Europe and the controversy with Arthur Lee.

Friday, Jan. 1, 1779

Commercial Committee 9 oClock. Congress Letters from G Gates to G Washington and answers relating the Canada Expidition   Letter from the

Delegate from New Jersey

Governor of Connecticut to their Delegates relating to the better allowance to Officers referrd to a Committee of 3 vizt. Mr Smith Mr Root & Mr Atley [Atlee]. Letter from Israil Ward of the State of New York, relating to his house being burnt by the Enemy, Referrd to a Committee of 3. vizt. Draton [Drayton], Burk [Burke], & Fell. Finance   President requested to invite Genl Washington to Dine[.] At 6 P M Commercial Committee

> Congress informed the minister of France and the Marquis de Lafayette that it sympathized with the plight of Canada and desired to see her independent. However, at the time neither Canada nor the United States was in a position to mount another invasion. The letter was from Stephen Ward, not Israil Ward.

Saturday, Jan. 2

9 oClock. Do [Commercial Committee]   11 A M Congress, Letter from Mr McDonald [John Donnell] of Salem County, complaining of not being paid for sundry goods taken by officers Referrd to a Committee Committee of 3. vizt. Roberdeau Root & Fell, Answerd Wards Letter, Mr Hopkinsons Sallery Voted 3500 Dolls. Preamble to the Finance Bill agreed to be printed   Dined with the So Carolina Delegates. City Tavern.

> Francis Hopkinson was Treasurer of Loans. The preamble to the finance bill was an

explanation of the current financial situation, the need for new taxes, and the necessity of calling in the previous bills of credit. Fell was not recorded as voting on the printing of the preamble.

Sunday, Jan. 3

moderate weather. (Chief Justice Morris in Town)

> This was Robert Morris, Chief Justice of New Jersey.

Monday, Jan. 4

Commercial Committee 9 oClock. Congress. Letter from Genl Sulevan [Sullivan] relating to a Court martial, Referrd to a Committee of 3. vizt. Drayton, Atley [Atlee] and Ellery. Letter from Mr Deane relating to Mr Paynes [Paine] adress, (Dined with Governeor [Gouverneur] Morris[)] 6 P M Commercial Committee.

> This was a continuation of the Deane-Lee controversy. Thomas Paine was a supporter of Lee.

Tuesday, Jan. 5

Do [Commercial Committee] 9 oClock. P M Dined wth Genl Washington. Congress Lievt Coll Fluerys [Fleury] Letter Read & debated Letter from Genl Schuyler with his Resignation to confer with Genl Washington on the subject carried in the negative. Proportion of the Taxes of Each State

New Hampshire	500,000
Masachusets	2,000,000
Rhode Island	300,000
Connecticut	1,700,000
New York	800,000
New Jersey	800,000
Pennsylvania	1,900,000
Delaware	150,000
Maryland	1,560,000
Virginia	2,400,000
No Carolina	1,090,000
So Carolina	1,800,000
Georgia	———
Dollars	15,000,000

NB Georgia being invaded pays no part of this Tax

> Colonel Fleury was a French officer serving in America. Congress stated that it would be happy to have his continued service. General Schuyler requested permission to resign because of personal financial reverses brought on by the war. His desire may have been motivated also by a dispute with General Gates. The figures listed here were the quotas for each state for the taxes to be paid in 1779.

The Journal

Wednesday, Jan. 6

Commercial Committee 9 oClock. Congress, Letter from Genl Sulevan [Sullivan] to Genl Washington Letter from Lt Browrigg [Brownrigg] to his Mother in Ireland, do [letter] from the State of Maryland respecting the Confederation, and approving of the alliance with France Letter from Thos Payne [Paine], Order for Mr Dunlap respecting printing a paper, Order for T Payne [Paine] whether he was the author, acknowledged himself the author and dismised, Debate ensued

> The Brownrigg letter was an intercepted letter sent by Sullivan to Washington. Under the name of "Common Sense" Paine authored a letter critical of Silas Deane in John Dunlap's newspaper. Dunlap identified Paine as the author, and Paine also admitted it. Congress then approved a resolution condemning articles dealing with foreign affairs and disclaimed any responsibility for them. The resolution also stated that Congress had never received military supplies from France as a gift and authorized a committee to investigate the truth of Paine's allegations. Apparently, French Minister Gerard was upset by the charges.

Thursday, Jan. 7

Commercial Committee 9 oClock. Letter read from Thos Payne [Paine] debate concerning him lasted all Day. Mr Thos Adams from Virginia[.] Dined with President Jay.

> The debate on the Paine matter continued. Various proposals were made to censure him for his action. Thomas Adams took his seat in Congress.

Friday, Jan. 8

Commercial Committee 9 oClock. Congress Letter read from T Payne [Paine] with his Resignation, debates on the subject lasted till past 4 oClock Dr Weatherspoon [Witherspoon] went home: Dined with Congress

> Paine resigned his office of Secretary to the Committee on Foreign Affairs. Paine's remark that he had seen the *Journals* from the day before was debated all day. Finally, after it was determined that Paine could not have seen them, Henry Laurens admitted that he had told Paine the details of the debate about him the previous day.

Saturday, Jan. 9

Commercial Committee 9 oClock. Congress Letter from Genl Putman [Putnam], giving an acct of Huntingtons Regement attempting to Mutiny, confind some and prevaild on the rest to return to their Duty, Referrd to the Committee to conferr with Genl Washington, Letters from Coll Beatty and Genl Portail were read referrd to the same

Committee; Coll Beatty wanted to have his powers defined, that he may act in his department of Commisary General of Prisoners, without being controld by the Officer on the Post &c. 2 Brigadier Generals appointed by Ballot for No Carolina viz Somner [Sumner] 13. Hogen [Hogun] 9. Clark 4. (? First[)] 1 Do [Brigadier General] for Maryland Coll Gist, Letter Read from Mr McPherson, desireing an appointment debate concerning Mr Payne [Paine] lasted till 5 P M.

> The nomination of Clark is not mentioned in the *Journals*. Colonels Huger, Sumner, and Hogun were elected. The question mark is in the original. The debate about Paine concerned the question of whether Congress intended to allow Paine to speak in his own defense before being removed from his position. Congress resolved that there was no intent to deny him a hearing.

Sunday, Jan. 10

Coll Scudder went home. Dined with Mr J. Searle.

Monday, Jan. 11

Commercial Committee 9 oClock. Congress. Debates concerning Mr Payne [Paine], and Mr Laurens motion about Mr Robt Morriss conduct in Shipping Tobacco. lasted till near 6 oClock.

> The debate about Paine continued. Robert Morris was accused of conducting private

commercial activities while holding public office and of using public ships to transport private goods.

Tuesday, Jan. 12

Commercial Committee 9 oClock. Congress. Lievt Hale [Hele] a prisoner Petion'd to go to New York. Referrd a Committee of 3 to draft a Letter to Admiral Gambier concerning him, Debates on Monsr Gerrard [Gerard] Memorial lasted till near 6 oClock. Letter from General Phillips to General Gates and Genl Washington & Lord Sterling [Stirling] Committee to conferr with Mr Gerrard [Gerard] about Flour to be Shipd Duane, Smith and Adams.

> Lieutenant Christopher Hele's letter is not recorded on this date in the *Journals*. There is a letter from him noted on January 7. Admiral Gambier had complained that Hele's imprisonment was a violation of the flag of truce. Gerard's memorial concerned the question of whether the goods sent by Deane from France were meant as gifts. This was the issue in which Paine had become involved. Congress assured Gerard that the goods were not considered as gifts and that Paine was not authorized to speak for Congress. Gerard also requested flour to supply French troops in America. Congress appointed the committee to investigate the matter.

The Journal

Wednesday, Jan. 13

Commercial Committee 9 oClock. Congress, Letter from Coll Grason [Grayson] with his Resignation reffer'd to the Committee to conferr with Genl Washington Sundry Letters from the Councill of Masachusetts Bay respecting Flour, and Securing the Harbour of Boston. Circular Letter Read to be sent to the Governors of Each State.

> The letter was an explanation of the financial situation and the necessity of calling in the bills of credit because of depreciation and counterfeiting.

Thursday, Jan. 14

Commercial Committee 9 oClock Congress. Debates relating to Monsr Girrards [Gerard] Letter. Letters from Genl Schuyler, relating to Indians and restoration to be made to sundry persons for damage Sustain'd by their forridge &c. Letters from Govr Clinton and Genl Washington in behalf of James Douel [McDowell] of Little Britain, for the Loss of his Barn &c. burnt by the Convention Troops, all Referrd to a Committee of 3 viz. Fell, Burk [Burke], & Dyer; Agreed to Emit 15000,400 Dollars.

> Gerard's letter concerned the rumor that the United States was considering concluding a separate peace with Britain. Congress resolved unanimously that such was not the case, and, in truth, the United States could

31

Delegate from New Jersey

not do so by the terms of its treaty with France. The figure listed here is incorrect; it should be $50,000,400.

Friday, Jan. 15

Commercial Committee 9 oClock. Congress. Letters from the Governors of Virginia and Maryland, advising of the Scheme agst Augustine being lay'd aside; Report from the Marine Committee to Reverse the Sentance of Capt McNeal [McNeil]. Memorial of Mr De Francy in behalf of Mr Bowmarcha [Beaumarchais] agreed to send him 3000 Hhds [hogsheads] Tobacco. At 6 P M at the Commercial Committee.

> The governors did not think their ships were in condition to move against St. Augustine. Hector McNeil was court-martialed for not aiding another ship in battle. The committee recommended that the guilty verdict be reversed, but the consideration was postponed and nothing was ever done about it. Mr. de Francy received the tobacco. He was the agent of Beaumarchais who was sent a letter of thanks from Congress on this date for his help in supplying the United States.

Saturday, Jan. 16

Congress. Resolved that the Committee for foreign affairs, order Mr Thos Payne [Paine] their Secretary to deliver on Oath, all the Papers &c. in his Office.

> Paine had already resigned, but the controversy continued to drag on. Fell is not recorded as voting on any of the measures this day.

Monday, Jan. 18

Commercial Committee 9 oClock 12 Went to Congress but not being States Sufficient no Congress At 6 P M Commercial Committee.

Tuesday, Jan. 19

Commercial Committee Excesive Cold. Congress. Letter from Genl Sulevan [Sullivan] to Genl Prescot [Prescott] and his answer. Do [letter] from Lt Coll Bradford for leave to Resign, Do [letter] from Capt Fowler late a British officer, Do [letter] from Genl Green [Greene] recomending Warrant Officers to have Commissions all referrd to the Board of Warr. Committee appointed on Acct of Mr Laurenss information against Mr R Morris viz. [blank]

> Fowler was later appointed auditor of the army. See entry for February 20. In order to settle the matter concerning Robert Morris (see notes for January 11) Congress appointed a committee to investigate the matter. Fell omits the names. They were Smith, Ellery, Ellsworth, Paca, and Thomas Adams.

Wednesday, Jan. 20

Commercial Committee 9 oClock. Congress. Letters from Seiur Gerrard [Gerard] & Genl De Portail and others. President requested, to answer them. Letter from Major Genl Lincoln with an acct of the Enemys taking Savanna in Georgia, Letter from Coll Ledwitz [Zedwitz] referrd to the Board of Warr. Letter from Genl McIntosh concerning the Indians referrd to Genl Washington. Letter from Mr Deane Motion for a Committee on foreign affairs one Member from Each State vizt. Whipple, Gerry, Ellery, Ellsworth Duane Fell, Searle, McKean Paca, Smith, Burk [Burke] Laurens, Langworthy.

> Apparently, the letter from Silas Deane and the continuing controversy with Arthur Lee prompted the creation of this committee to conduct foreign affairs and to investigate the conduct of former and present American commissioners in Europe.

Thursday, Jan. 21

Commercial Committee 9 oClock. Congress, Letter from the French Minister, and the Marine Committees answer about Provision, and the Commissary Generals reply that he could not furnish any Flour to the Minister. 6 P M Commercial Committee.

> This was in answer to Gerard's request for flour on January 12. The answer was that

the request could not be met without causing hardship to American troops.

Friday, Jan. 22

Do . . . . Do [Commercial Committee] 9 oClock till 3 P M Congress. . Coll Frelinghuysen came to town today but I did not go to Congress. Coll Cadwalader Resign'd President to write to the Governors of South and North Carolina to assist Georgia. President to write to the Count Estang [d'Estaing] to request his assistance and to send two advice Boats and the Marquis of Britagnie [de Bretigny] to have the Command of one, Letter from Commisary Jeremiah Wadsworth against the Distilling of Grain refferd to a Committee, Genl Washingtons Letter reccomending Coll Rawlinss [Rawlings] 3 Companys to be recuted. Letter from General Phillips, Letter from Count Mumford [Montfort] for leave to Resign granted. Committee on Col Beattys Letter Reported that the Commisary General of Prisoners, Reside at Camp and that he receive orders from the Commander in Chief, Congress, or the Board of Warr. Inspector General to have the Rank of Major General.

> Frelinghuysen was a new delegate from New Jersey. The letter was also to request aid for South Carolina. Beginning with Wadsworth's letter, these entries should have been made on January 23. See Fell's next entry. Wadsworth stated that since

distilling was illegal in Pennsylvania, distillers were moving into Maryland and would possibly cause a shortage of bread. General Phillips, a British officer, was denied parole because of the treatment of American prisoners in New York.

Saturday, Jan. 23

Commercial Committee 9 oClock. Congress. Introduced Coll Frelinghuysen.
NB some of the Business sett down Yesterday was done this day and Enterd thro mistake.

Monday, Jan. 25

Commercial Committee 9 oClock. Congress Motion to call Robt Lettice Hooper to acct. for having several Brigades of Continental Waggons Loaded with Flour and Iron, on Private account the General requested to call a Court Martial; Bounty of 20 Dolls besides the 80 offerd before with Land and Cloathing and to the Officer for Inlisting 10 Ds at Camp and 20 abroad and 3 Ds a Day, Wm Bedlow, auditor Committee on Genl Lincolns Letter, Laurens, Root & Lee. Johnson [Johnston] Smiths complaint agst Coll Flowers at Carlisle Committee Roberdieu [Roberdeau], Dyer & Hill. 6 P M Committee on foreign affairs Mr Whipple Chairman

> There is no mention in the *Journals* of Hooper, but there was a motion for "reme-

dying the abuses in the several public departments." The matter of bounties is recorded on January 23. The bounty for re-enlistment was not to exceed $200. Recruiting officers were to receive not more than $10 for each soldier and $20 for each officer who re-enlisted. They were to receive $3 per day for expenses. Bedlow was nominated on January 23 for auditor of the army. Lincoln's letter concerned his command in the South. On March 23 the committee on Smith's complaint against Col. Flowers reported that it could find no evidence of wrongdoing by Flowers in his position of purchasing goods for public use.

Tuesday, Jan. 26

Commercial Committee 9 oClock. Congress, Letter from President Read [Reed] in Council complaining of Major Genl Arnolds conduct in useing publick Waggons in private affairs &c and of Indignity to their Body Referrd to a Committee of 5 vizt. Paca, Burk [Burke], Floyd, Holton [Holten] & Root. Instructions read to the Delegates of Pensylvania, complaining of an improper arrangement in their State of Brigadier Generals, Referrd to the above Committee 6 P M attended the Committee on foreign affairs a most miserable Rainy bad Night.

>Reed was President of Pennsylvania. Fell constantly misspells his name. Benedict

Delegate from New Jersey

Arnold, the Continental commander of Philadelphia, regularly provoked the Pennsylvania authorities by what they considered to be his outrageous conduct. Pennsylvania also complained that it did not have enough brigadier generals.

Wednesday, Jan. 27

Commercial Committee 9 oClock. Congress Sundry Letters read, Long debates about the Marquis of Britagnies [de Bretigny] Instructions 6 P M Committee on foreign affairs.

> Marquis de Bretigny was commissioned a lieutenant in the American army and was to carry instructions to the Comte d'Estaing.

Thursday, Jan. 28

Commercial Committee 9 oClock. Letter from Genl Lincoln, with 1400 Continental & Militia, Enemy Genl Campbell 4000, Letter from Genl How [Howe] with 600. Letter from Govr Lounds [Lowndes] desiring Frigates to be sent to So Carolina; Debate on the french Ministers proposal for Compensation if Count Estang [d'Estaing] goes to Georgia. 6 P M Committee on foreign affairs

Friday, Jan. 29

Commercial Committee 9 oClock. Congress Letter from David Franks for leave for his Clerk to go to New York, Letter from G Washington for leave

The Journal

to go to Camp, Motion for the defence of Georgia and So Carolina debated. Referrd to the Committee to conferr with the General Letter from the President Read, in answer to the Minister of France for his request of Compensation, long debate lasted till near 5 oClock

> Washington requested that his attendance at Congress be ended and that he be allowed to return to the field.

Saturday, Jan. 30

Letters Read from Govr Clinton and Genl Washington for the payment of Sundry people in the State of New York, Letter read from Genl DePortail relating to the fortyfying Boston Harbour, referr'd to the Marine Committee Brigr Hamiltons Letter to Coll Harvey [Harvie] in Virginia and his answer, relating to the accomodation of the Convention Troops.

> This was payment for goods taken by the army from private citizens.

Monday, Feb. 1

Commercial Committee Letter from Chevalier [de] Cambray going to So Carolina to put the fortifications in order. Genl Washington apply'd for leave to return to Camp came and took his leave of Congress. Letter from the Assembly of Masachussets Bay, to request the Embargo be taken off in order to Import grain to the Eastward, also a complaint from Rhode Island of the great want of Flour and other provisions the Inhabitants being in a Starving condition, Referrd to a Committee of 5. vizt. Dyer, Ellery, Paca Laurens and Floyd. Memorial of Sundry People in Phila. acquainting of a Number of Privateers on the Coast and if Congress will sell one of their Frigates they will fitt her out for the protection of Trade; Motion for Selling the 2 Frigates on the 1st of March Committed to the Marine Committee. Letter from Gl Washington relating to Genl McIntosh for want of Provisions at Fort Pitt. the General to arrange the Quarter Masters and Commisary department to the Westward. President Reads [Reed] complaint agst M Clarkson, orderd that he not leave the City till he has satisfied the Council 6 P M Committee on foreign affairs.

> Because Clarkson, aide-de-camp to Benedict Arnold, refused to obey the summons of the President and Executive Council of Pennsylvania, he was considered very disrespectful to that body.

Tuesday, Feb. 2

Commercial Committee 9 oC. Congress. Motion for Powder Shot & Armes to be sent to So Carolina by Coll Cambra [Cambray], that the General [Washington] send an Engenier to So Carolina, Letter from Gl Gates—Letter from do [Gates] to

Genl Washington. Letter from Gl Green [Greene] reccomending a plan for setling the account of people who have sufferd damage by the army. Referrd to the Committee to consult with the Quarter Master General Board of Warr to contract with Monsr Penet &c for Fire Arms &c. Report Read from the Committee of Appeals. At 6 P M attended the Committee on foreign affairs but not members enough, did no Business.

Wednesday, Feb. 3

Commercial Committee. Congress. After agreeing to Count Polaskey [Pulaski] & Coll Armand, Cores of Infantry to recruted, Went in to Committee of the whole House Resolved that 500,160 [5,000,160] Dollars in Certificates be Prepaird for Exchanging the Emisions to be call'd in, debates lasted till 5 P M. 6 P M Committee on foreign affairs.

> The recruiting of infantry is recorded in the *Journals* under February 4.

Thursday, Feb. 4

Commercial Committee. Watkins Commissary of Purchases with his Resignation Referrd to the Board of Warr. Resolved that the Commander in Chief arrange the Relative Rank of Officers, under the degree of Brigadr Generals. (committed to the Board of Warr) Letter from Mr Bingham at Martinico [Martinique], giving an account of the

British taking the Island of St Luica and of Count Delstangs [d'Estaing] repulse in endeavoring to retake it. 6 P M. Committee on foreign affairs.

> Watkins was Commissary of Ordnance and Military Stores. The report stated that no commission would be given if the applicant had not first contacted the Board of War.

Friday, Feb. 5

Commercial Committee 9 oClock. Congress Letter from Count Polaska [Pulaski], referrd to the Board of Warr, Do [letter] from Coll Armand, that as he cannot be Promoted, he desires to go to France. Granted. Letter from the Marquis Fayatt [de Lafayette] he Saild from Boston on the 14 Jany in the Alliance and his dispatches did not get there till the 15th. Committee appointed to write to the Marquis to acquaint him the Expidition to Canada was set aside. Letter from Governor Hueston [Houstoun] at Georgia, and President Lounds [Lowndes] at So Carolina Jany 15 long debate about the manner of wording the request to the French Minister for the Aid of Count Delstang [d'Estaing] for the Relief of Georgia. 6 P M. Committee on foreign Affairs.

Saturday, Feb. 6

Commercial Committee 9 oClock Long debates about the manner of sending for Count Delstang [d'Estaing] Congress agreed to Dine at the City

Tavern being the aniversary of the French Alliance.

> The *Journals* do not mention the discussion of d'Estaing on this date.

Monday, Feb. 8

Commercial Committee 9 oClock. Congress. a number of Letters Read; A Memorial from Lt Coll Varick in behalf of himself and the Officers in the Muster Masters department Referrd to the Board of Warr, A Memorial from Dr Shippen in behalf of himself and the other Doctors, Referrd to the Medical Committee, Long debates again about sending to Count Delstang [d'Estaing] &c. 6 P M Committee on foreign affairs.

Tuesday, Feb. 9

Commercial Committee Congress. a Number of Letters. a Curious one from Philip Johnson with offers to destroy the Fly that does so much hurt to the Wheat. Card to the President, from M Gerrard [Gerard], Treasury appointed 5 auditors —Wm Bedlow appointed one. Committee appointed to examine the accusation agst Robt Morris Reported 6 P M Committee on foreign affairs.

> The letter from Johnson was probably really from P. Jackson, as recorded in the *Journals*. The report on Morris concerned

his possible use of public ships for private ventures.

Wednesday, Feb. 10

Commercial Committee Congress Letters Read Mr Morriss Defence and papers Read. Deferd till Tuesday next, President Reeds Letters & Major Clarksons, Debate lasted till 5 oClock.

Thursday, Feb. 11

Commercial Committee. Congress Sundry Letters read and Referrd to Committee Aron [Aaron] Lopezs Memorial relating to 2 Prizes, Referrd to the Committee of Appeals, Memorial of Capt Cellorine [Celeron] to the Board of Warr. do [memorial] of Sarah Kennedy for the loss of her Estate, Referrd to the Treasury Board. Letter from Genl Gates wth an acct of the Enemy at several posts in Canada 2952 above Montreal 3922 Letter from Jeremiah Powell President of Masachusets Bay giving an acct of Coll David Mason and others great defaulters of the Public Money at the Labratory at Springfield Referrd to the Commander in Chief, to bring the defaulters to a Court Martial; Mr Laurens moved the House that he was fully satisfied in the affair relating to Mr R Morris, and declared him clear of all Suspicion to which the House unanamously agreed, An order from the Treasury for Coll Flowerss department causd great debate and his Carractor Canvasd which appeared good.

> Fell's figures on troop strength are incorrect. One group had 2,952 men and another 970. The total was 3,922. Fell's comments about Montreal are not clear. David Mason, deputy commissary-general of military stores at Springfield, was court-martialed and the results were transmitted to Congress (see *Journals,* April 14). Apparently, the Morris controversy was settled; a long letter from him is printed in the *Journals.* See entry and notes for January 25 on the Flowers issue.

Friday, Feb. 12

Commercial Committee Congress Letter from R Curson and others at Baltimore referr'd to the Marine Committee, Lievt Hales [Hele] Letter[.] Genl Polaskas [Pulaski] Letter to Recruit his Infantry to their full Establishment not agreed to.

> Curson's letter was from a group of Baltimore merchants. Hele's letter concerned his imprisonment (see note for January 12). Congress stated that Pulaski's infantry should be returned to its original size.

Saturday, Feb. 13

Commercial Committee Congress. Coll Hartleys Resignation accepted Resolv'd that Congress have a high Sence of the Services renderd his Country.

Great and long debates about the Mode of Receiving Mr Gerrard [Gerard] to a Conferrence agreed to be on Monday 1. oClock in Committee of the whole House. Dined with Mr R Morris

Sunday, Feb. 14.

(Very Hott weather)

Monday, Feb. 15

Commercial Committee Congress. Conferance with Mr Gerrard [Gerard] 6 P M. Committee on foreign affairs.

Tuesday, Feb. 16

Commercial Committee 9 oC Congress. Great debates relating to Genl Arnold, a motion for Suspending him, agreed to Postpone the motion till the Committee brought in their Report. A Representation from the Assembly of Pennsylvania to their Delegates in Congress, Relating to the Distresses of the Frontier Inhabitants, Letter from Govr. Clinton of New York, and one from Govr Turnbull [Trumbull], Connecticut all to the same purport. Referrd to the Committee of Conferrence Letter from the Govr of Virginia concerning the Convention Troops, referrd to their Delegates Corn £10 to £15 by Barrell Dined with Coll Griffin.

> This was a part of the continuing controversy between Benedict Arnold and the

government of Pennsylvania. The reference to corn is apparently the current price. Cyrus Griffin was a delegate from Virginia.

Wednesday, Feb. 17

Commercial Committee Congress Memorial Read from all the Officers now Prisoners on Long Island praying to be Exchanged refferd to a Committee of 3. vizt. Duane, Atley [Atlee] & Dyer Widdow Kennedys Report, and Treasury Board opinion thereon postponed. Sundry foreign Letters from Arther Lee & other Commisioners & from John Ross were Read G Morris moved with many Reasons well drawn up that the above Letters, and the late Conferrence with the Minister be Referrd to a special Committee agreed to 5 vizt. Morris, Burk [Burke], Weatherspoon [Witherspoon] S Adams, and Smith. Secret 6 P M. Committee on foreign affairs only 3

> Sarah Kennedy's request for compensation for damage done to her property by Continental soldiers was reported upon. A decision was postponed.

Thursday, Feb. 18

Commercial Committee Congress Letter from President Powell & one from Coll Ward, on Long Island, in behalf of the Prisoners on Long Island, Referrd to the Committee appointed yesterday, Barron Stewbon [Steuben] the Inspector Generals

Rules and orders, application from the Board of Warr for a further allowance, agreed 84 Dolls in addition to his pay as a Major General, Letter from Count Polaska [Pulaski]. Report of New Regulations in the Artilery Line &c. 6 P M. Committee on foreign affairs   Only 3 Members

> Powell was President of Massachusetts Bay. There was a new "Plan for the Department of Inspector General" which allowed Baron von Steuben as Inspector General to receive the extra pay. There was also a new "Arrangement of the Department of Ordnance" reported.

Friday, Feb. 19

Commercial Committee   Congress. President Reeds Letter, requesting the Resolutions of Congress with regard to sundry officers therein mentiond, On motion that he should have applied to the Delegates of the State, caused long debates Letter from the Board of Warr, setting forth the necesity of putting the Clothier Generals Business on a better footing, and also the exceeding bad management of the Commisary of Hides department; the first Referrd to the Committee of Conferrence, and the last relating Hides to the Bd. of Warr to Report   The Treasury requested a New Emission of 5,160000 [5,000,160] and also their reasons for not complying with the request of the Commercial Committee for 500,000 Ds. President

The Journal

acquainted the House that the Minister of France had told him, that his health was Impaird and he beleived the air of this Country did not agree with him, that he had leave to go to France, and that another was appointed in his Room. A Frigate was orderd to be imediatly prepaird to carry him Home. This night the Committee did not meet. Rainy night

> President Reed of Pennsylvania requested information on Pennsylvania officers. No mention is made in the *Journals* of Gerard's plan to leave. The Marine Committee was ordered, however, to prepare a frigate for sea at once.

Saturday, Feb. 20

Commercial Committee   Letter from John Hart, relating to his Loss by Cloth taken from his fulling Mill, Committee of 3. Vizt. Dyer, Hill & Weatherspoon [Witherspoon]. Letter from Capt Hector McNeal [McNeil] to be considerd on Tuesday. Memorial of Lucy DePasey [Lewis D. Passern]. Board of Warr do [memorial] from Capt Celleron, to have a Brevet for the Rank of Major. No. Motion to allow him 1000 Ds. agreed   Ay.   Petition from Timothy Pening [Penny] to send a Vessell to Jamaica, referrd to a Committee vizt. Adams, Dyer, & Collins. Report read about the Convention Troops in Virginia   2 Auditors appointed for the Army. vizt. Varley and Powell   Motion for

Delegate from New Jersey

Pay Master and Treasurer for the Marine Board, deferrd. Motion for 100,000 Ds. for the Commercial Committee, Motion for the Officers to be furnishd by the Quarter Master, with Portmantuas [Portmanteaus], and Valances [Valeses] at the Publick Expence.

> Celeron, a foreign officer, had requested money and a promotion. The auditors appointed were Felix Varley and Alexander Fowler.

Sunday, Feb. 21

Fine Pleasant Weather.

Monday, Feb. 22

Rain Commercial Committee Congress, Letters from A Lee at Paris Letter from Wm Bingham Agent at Martinico by the Revenge Cutter wth one Case of Tea & 50 Chests of Arms, long debate abt the Forign Committee A Lee beleives the British Commissioners have orders to acknowledge our Independcy.

> A. Lee's letter was probably the one recorded in the *Journals* from William Lee with the draft of a treaty of commerce between Holland and the United States.

Tuesday, Feb. 23

Commercial Committee Congress. Sundry Letters Read. Committee of Conferrance with Mr

Gerrard [Gerard] brought in a Report, after long debate agreed to consider on the Report on Thursday in a Committee of the whole House 6 P M. Committee on foreign affairs

Wednesday, Feb. 24

Commercial Committee Congress. Letters from the Commissioners at Paris to know the Colours used by the different States referrd to the Marine Committee, And also how to treat with Algerines [Count de Vergennes], Referrd to Mr Carmichael, Nelson & Burk [Burke]. Members chose to fill up the Marine Committee vizt., for Virginia R. H. Lee Pennsylvania Mr Searle New Jersey Mr Fell Treasury Board Mr Frelinghuysen, Committee on foreign affairs Mr Dyer, A Soldier Condemned by a Court Martial, Pardoned. President Reeds Letter and papers relating to Major Clarkson Read, and several motions made respecting him, occasiond long debates till past 5.

> The colors were requested so that the King of Naples, who had opened his ports to Americans, would be able to recognize American ships. The soldier was Patrick Roach, who was to have been executed for desertion. Congress expressed its displeasure with Clarkson's attitude and actions toward the government of Pennsylvania.

Thursday, Feb. 25

Commercial Committee Congress Letter from

Major Genl Mifflin desireing leave to Resign his Commission, after long debate it was accepted. At the Request of the Assembly for the State of Pensylvania, agreed to Raise 5 Companys of 73 Men Each for the defence of the Western Frontiers the acct to be transmitted to the Commander in Chief Dr Wetherspoon [Witherspoon] went home

> The companies were to be enlisted for nine months. Each volunteer would receive a bounty of $100 and Continental pay and rations, but he had to provide his arms and clothing at his own expense.

Friday, Feb. 26

Commercial Committee Congress. Letter from G Lee to Negoiate in N York some Bills of Excha. for Gold to purchase Negroes Vote pas'd in the Negative. Report for Masachusets & Rhode Island, to send for Flour to the Southern States, agreed under Restrictions of their several Governors &c. 6 P M, Attended the Committee on foreign affairs. agreed to Mr Laurens, Mr Paca, Mr Burk [Burke], drawing a Report.

> There is no mention in the *Journals* of Lee's desire to purchase Negroes.

Saturday, Feb. 27

Commercial Committee Congress. Letter from G Lee, Referrd to the Treasury Board. Order of

The Journal

the Day. The house went in to a Committee of the whole. Coll Frelinghuysen went home

> The Committee of the Whole was to discuss foreign affairs.

Sunday, Feb. 28

Fine warm Pleasant Day.

Monday, Mar. 1

Commercial Committee   Letter from Genl Washington, inclosing one from Genl Maxwell at Elizabethtown, that the Enemy had left that place, after a fruitless Incursion. Memorial from Mr Holker offering a Million of Dolls on Loan   Referrd to Mr R. H. Lee, Laurens & Morris, Committee of the Assembly of Pennsylvania, desire a Conferrence with a Committee of Congress, relating to the Emitions call'd out of Circulation, Gerry, Carmichael, Duane. Motion for the Committee to whom was Referrd the Letters & Papers from President Reed &c. be Requir'd to send and Examine on oath Mr Mitchell D Q M Gener, respecting the Waggons, said to be employd by Genl Arnold. Congress went in to a Committee of the whole House, Respecting the fixing of Bounderies of the United States.

> Holker, a Frenchman, apparently made the offer at the suggestion of the King of France. The third member of the com-

mittee was Meriwether Smith, not Morris. The questioning of Mitchell was a continuation of the dispute between Pennsylvania and Benedict Arnold.

Tuesday, Mar. 2

Commercial Committee Congress. some Letters read and a Memorial from the Board of Warr, about clothing the army Report for Raising a Lone in Europe, and the Properity of Paying Beaumarchies [Beaumarchais] Debt, debated till 4 oClock. 6 P M. Attended the Marine Committee (first time[)]

Wednesday, Mar. 3

Commercial Committee Congress. This day spent in Debates, on the Report of the Committee on Appeals, The State of Pennsylvania being of Opinion the Court of Appeals, Establishd by Congress, had no authority over Courts of Admiralty where the Jury were Judges of Facts, Congress say they have a Right of Sovereignity in all Admiralty affairs whatsoever in the last Resort.

> These debates were in the Committee of the Whole.

Thursday, Mar. 4

Commercial Committee Congress. went in to a Committee of the whole house, to consider the

The Journal

Boundery Lines to be fixt for an Ultimatom, Adjourn'd till tomorrow   6 P M. Marine Committee

Friday, Mar. 5

Commercial Committee   Congres. Report from the Board of Warr, Recomend a Mode of Payment, to the Inhabitants, for what has being taken from them by Officers in the Army agreed to be publish'd, A Report from a Committee to empower the Commander in Chief, to setle a Cartel with the British General for the Exchange of Prisoners, for the Convention Troops, or others as he may Judge Best. A number of Letters Read &c. 6 P M. Marine Committee. £62456.

> The meaning of the figures at the end is a mystery.

Saturday, Mar. 6

Com Committee   Congress   Committee of 3 to conferr with a Committee of the State of Pennsylvania relating to the Court of Appeals. Several Memorials, Letter &c. A Warrant for 500,000 Ds for the use of Commercial Committee to procure Cloathing for the Army.

> This dispute with Pennsylvania, simmering for some time, actually concerned sovereignty. The question of jurisdiction was ultimately one of power. The specific question at hand was not significant; the resolution of the basic question was of supreme

55

importance. The committee appointed consisted of Paca, Burke, and R. H. Lee.

Sunday, Mar. 7

Last night, Snow, and this morning Cold & verry disagreeable.

Monday, Mar. 8

Commercial Committee   Congress. Speaker of the Assembly of the State of Pennsylvanias Letter to Borrow money for the use of the State, Referrd to a Committee of 3. Letters from Genl Washington, Govr Turnbull [Trumbull] &c. Report of the Committee concerning Lievt Hale [Hele] and the crew of the Hotham— & a Letter to Adml Gambier

> Plater, Dyer, and Nelson were appointed to the committee.

Tuesday, Mar. 9

Commercial Committee   This day chiefly spent on the Report, for Recruting the Army of 80 Batallions. 6 P M Marine Committee.

> The eighty battalions were apportioned among the states according to population.

Wednesday, Mar. 10

Commercial Committee   Congress. After the Treasury Reports, being Read Went in to a Committee of the whole House, on fixing a Boundery Line to the Missasipy   7 for 5 agst. No.

The Journal

The question of the western boundary was a delicate one. Apparently Fell did not approve, although a majority of the states did. Since this action was taken by the Committee of the Whole, there is no recorded vote in the *Journals*.

Thursday, Mar. 11

Commercial Committee Congress. Went in a Committee of the whole House, That if our allies would Support us, we should Insist on Novia Scotia being declar'd Independant, Long debate No. carried in the affirmitive. 6 P M Marine Committee, Dined with Mr Jay NB. Coll Frelinghuysen Came to Congress

> This action concerning Nova Scotia seems to be a reversal of a decision on February 23.

Friday, Mar. 12

Commercial Committee Congress. Letters from Major Genl Lincoln, with proposals of Exchange of Prisoners, between his Officer and Lievt. Coll Prevost, Referrd to a Committee of 3. Report of the Committee on the Business of setling the payment of Goods taken from several persons in Phila. agreed to pay them at the then Current price when taken. Long Debate. 6 P M Marine Committee.

Saturday, Mar. 13

Spent this day at the Commercial Committee.

Sunday, Mar. 14

Snow.

Monday, Mar. 15

Commercial Committee Congress Letter from Genl Washington and Genl Maxwell, Imagine Admiral Gambier is going to New London. Genl Putman [Putnam] has sent 400 Men there, Letter from Mr Deane, Long debate, the Committee on forreign affairs to Report on Friday. Congress went in a Committee of the whole House to consider Bounds &c.

Tuesday, Mar. 16

Commercial Committee Congress. After Reading Letters &c. Went in to a Committee of the whole house, to consider of Bounderies &c. 6 P M Marine Committee.

Wednesday, Mar. 17

Commercial Committee Congress Motion to Publish the acct. that the King of the 2 Scisellys [Sicilies] would open his Ports for the Vesells of the United States, And also to Publish as much of the Information from the french Minister as is necessary for the Public to be acquainted with. Report of the Committee on Genl Arnolds affair postponed till Monday. Letter from the Speaker of the Assembly for the Loan of 2 Million of

Dollars. Committee of the whole to take in to consideration the Bounderies &c. 6 P M met the Committee on foreign affairs.

> There is no mention of the King of the Two Sicilies in the *Journals*. The committee on Arnold read its report, but consideration was deferred. The Committee of the Whole made its report on peace terms, but consideration was postponed.

Thursday, Mar. 18

Commercial Committee Congress. Letter from Genl Washington Reccomending a better plan for Cloathing and Recruting the Army. Letter from Genl Schuyler to Resign, 7 No 5 Ay Negative Report from the Committee, to the Request from Pennsylvania that the Treasury could not comply with their Request Memorial Read from Mr Girrard [Gerard]. 6 P M Committee on foreign affairs.

> The substance of Gerard's memorial was to encourage Congress to decide quickly what its peace demands were to be.

Friday, Mar. 19

Com Committee Congress. Sundry Letters Read. Went in to the Consideration of the sundry articles agreed for an Ultimatom in setling Bounderies, long debates till 4. 6 P M Attended the Marine Committee

Congress agreed upon the demands for the boundaries of the United States and the immediate evacuation by the British of the entire area.

Saturday, Mar. 20

Commercial Committee Congress. Letters from General How [Howe], Govr Rutledge So Carolina, Govr Henry of Virginia. Report of G Morris for a Fast, to be on the first Thursday in May.

Sunday, Mar. 21

Dined with Mr J Searle (Rain all night)

Monday, Mar. 22

Commercial Committee. Congress. Order of the Day, for considering the Ultimatum for the Fishery, Long Debate. Report for appointing Clothier General &c. to be considered to morrow morning. 6 P M Committee on forreign affairs.

> The rights to fish off Newfoundland and Nova Scotia and to use the coast for curing fish were under consideration. Congress agreed to demand the fishing rights.

Tuesday, Mar. 23

Commercial Committee. Congress, went in to the Report of having a Clothier General &c. &c. Letter Read from Major Clarkson for leave to go to the Southern Army., Motion made by one of the

The Journal

Delegates for Pennsylvania, that he have leave to go. long debate, Motion to postpone Yeas & Nas call'd for carried in the affirmitive. Motion by Gr. Morris that Major Clarkson be calld to the Barr and Repremanded by the Chair for his past conduct in writing disrespectfull Letters to the Execitive Council of this State &c. 6 P M Marine Committee.

> Congress decided to appoint a Clothier-General.

Wednesday, Mar. 24

Commercial Committee Congress. Letter from Majr Clarkson Read in which he seems to doubt the authority of Congresss power to send for him, At 12 He came and was Reprimanded. After he was discharg'd, it was moved that a Brivet Commission of Major be given him, after much debate the mover withdrew the Motion Order of the Date for considering the Bounderies, Line to be drawn in Latd 45. agreed, Gave my Negative to the full and free Navigation of the Missasipia, if we must continue the Warr for that to be our Ultimatom. Na. NB a very great storm of Snow

> The matter of the brevet commission is not recorded in the *Journals*. Fell voted with the majority to reject the demand for free navigation of the Mississippi. See notes for March 30. There is some confusion about the votes actually taken this day.

Thursday, Mar. 25

Commercial Committee Congress. Debates abt. the Clothier Generals department, postponed till to morrow, A Report from the Delegates of So Carolina & Georgeia, for Raising [blank] Battalions of Negroes to be Officerd by White Men and appointed by the authority of the State, to be allowd 1000 Dolls for Ea NB. This morning Coll Freilinghuysen [Frelinghuysen] went home. 6 P M Marine Committee.

> The *Journals* record that rules for the clothing department were approved on March 23. No mention is made of this on this date.

Friday, Mar. 26

Commercial Committee Congress. Letters, from the Chairman of a Committee of the Assembly & Execitive Council of Pennsylvania desireing a Conferrance with a Committee of Congress, Motion for Commiting the papers Ys 5. Ns 5, 2 devided, 1 not Represented. Motion by G Morris that a Committee be appointed agreeable to the Request Mr Smith moved as an amendmant the Committee of Council be struck out. Long debate 5 Ys Ns 5. then ensuid a long debate on order till Adjournd an unhappy dispute, Occasiond intirely by means of Major General Arnold. 6 P M Marine Committee.

The Journal

The one state not represented was New Jersey. Fell voted to commit the request. This controversy was a continuation of the question of Arnold's command at Philadelphia.

Saturday, Mar. 27

Commercial Committee Congress. Letter from Major Genl Arnold requesting the Report of the Committee to be taken up, on which the Report was Read, and the papers Letters &c. that pased between the Committee and the Execitive Council after which a Motion was made that Genl Arnolds affair be postponed, and the Motion of Yesterday taken in to consideration for a Committee to meet a Committee of the Assembly and a Committee of the Execetive Council in Conferrance Ys & Ns Carrd in the affirmitive, then M Smith moved after a long Speech, that the Chair be requested to call on Each Member to know if they have Receiv'd any inteligence from any foreign Court, in Europe and particularly from England Ys & Ns carrd in the affirmitive. All No Mr Lovell moved for Mr Aken [Aitken] to Print the Journals debate about the propriety of Printing the Yas & Nas &c. the Ys & Ns calld for on the Question carrd in the affirm. I was No. I think they are very often Ridicolous.

>Apparently, all members reported that they had received no intelligence from Europe. The *Journals* only record the motion and

vote; there is nothing on the answers. The *Journals* mention nothing about Aitken as printer of the *Journals*.

Monday, Mar. 29

Coml Committee Congress. Motion for taking in to consideration the Raising Negroes Troops in So Carolina & Georgia Repeal of the Resolve relating to the Bahama Islands Motion for appointing the Committee of Conferrence, with the Execitive Council & Assembly of Pennsilvania, a Motion by Mr Smith of a very extraordinary nature Respecting himself and the Commercial Committee, Over Ruled. Committee appointed to conferr, Mr Paca, Root R H Lee S Adams, & Mr Laurens NB Motion that all the Members of Congress now in Town may be Requested to attend this House at 10 oClock [blank] on [blank] Morning, to Consult and endeavour to fix a proper Plan for Raising the Credt of Our Money. Not secconded.

> The committee reported that the matter of guarding Negroes in Georgia and South Carolina and the possibility of slave insurrection, especially encouraged by the British, were causing trouble in those states. Congress decided to recommend to the states the possibility of raising 3,000 black soldiers for defense and control of other slaves. If the state approved, the troops would be officered by whites in sepa-

rate units and Congress would compensate owners not to exceed $1,000 per slave; the slaves would not be paid but would be clothed and fed by the national government, and those who served well and faithfully would receive emancipation and fifty dollars at the end of the war. Smith accused the Commercial Committee of being weak, inefficient, and disgraceful. He requested that he be excused from serving on this committee.

Tuesday, Mar. 30

Commercial Committee Congress. A Number of Letters, and one from Mr Gerrard [Gerard] to hasten the Plan for Treaty, Agreed to an Ultimatum for the Fishery, which I am afraid will involve us in a Continuance of the Warr. Motion by R H Lee 6 Ays 5 Nos 1 devided 1 not Represented NB New Jersey 6 P M Marine Committee

> There is reason to believe that the last vote recorded on March 24 was erroneously listed in the *Journals.* Instead of March 24, it should have been included for March 30. See notes for March 24.

Wednesday, Mar. 31

Commercial Committee Congress. A Letter from Thos Payne [Paine] Read A do [letter] from Govr Trumbull, to setle his Brothers accts. Committee on Commissary Trumbulls accts Reported that his Estate be allow'd as follows to wit

Delegate from New Jersey

½ Per Ct. on all the Moneys laid out, Yas & Nas carrd affirmitive

2½ Per Ct. on all purchases made by himself do [Yas & Nas] ... do [affirmitive]

½ Per Ct. on all the Money lay'd out do [Yas & Nas] even Lost

not finish'd   Motion made by Mr Smith that Mr [blank] be appointed Printer for the Public and that the Journals be printed in Sheets and sent to the Legislatures of the different States   Dr Wetherspoon [Witherspoon]

> The death of Commissary Trumbull caused much confusion. This was an attempt to make a fair financial settlement. No mention is made in the *Journals* of Smith's motion.

Thursday, April 1

Com Committee   Congress, Letter from Genl Washington, Do [letter] from Leivt Coll Ledwitz [Zedwitz], Referrd to the Board of Warr. Letter from Lt Govr & Speaker of the Assembly of New York to Raise 1000 Men for a Western Expiditon against the Indians agreed. Memorial from A Edwards, to Join the Southern Army, Bd of Warr. Leivt Coll Bradford & Lt Coll [Yeates] Muster Masters have leave to Resign & nominated H. Rutgars [Rutgers] Esqr. and [blank] in their Room. Report from the Board of Warr to appoint a Clothier General with a Sallery of 10,000 Dolls

The Journal

by annum to have 12 Rations, and forrege for 3 Horses. Postponed. Governor Trunbulls [Trumbull], proposal for taking Sailsbury [Salisbury] Iron Works, not agreed to, Mr Whiteing [Whiting] to be paid his Expenses by the Treasury Board. Report from the Treasury Board for an Emission of 5,000160 Ds. Mr Paca informd Congress of what pasd at the Conferrence with President Reed Accounts from New York, say that have taken to the Soward Genl Egbert [Elbert], Coll McIntosh, 33 Officers, 300 Prisoners, 300 Field and 7 Peices Cannon. NB Marine Committee did not meet

> Congress agreed to financially support the New York expedition against the Indians. The letter was from Evan Edwards, not A. Edwards. The name Yeates was written into a blank space in pencil in a handwriting other than Fell's. The *Journals* show the correct name to be Noarth instead of Yeates. The other Muster Master was Azariah Horton. Trumbull requested that Congress take over the Salisbury furnace to manufacture cannon. A negative report made after conferring with Mr. Whiting, an expert cannon maker, was accepted by Congress.

Friday, April 2

Commercial Committee This being Good Fryday. Congress met an adjourn'd. NB. Marine Committee did not make a Board.

Delegate from New Jersey

Saturday, April 3

Commercial Committee Congress. Letter from Commissary General of Prisoners to Exchange Leivt Hale [Hele]. Letter from Capt Willing to be Exchangd Refer'd to the Marine Committee. Board of Warr Reccomend Lt Coll Fleury and 3 others to a gratuity of 1000, 600, 500 & 400 Dolls. not allowd Motion for taking in to consideration the Report of the Committee on foreign affairs on Tuesday next in consequence of a Letter from Mr Deane. Board of Warr Reported that 12 Commissions be sent to Major Genl Schuyler for the friendly Indians agreed. An Inspector to be appointed for the Batallions of Negroes to be Raisd in South Carolina and Georgia. No. A very impertinent Letter from Thos. Payne [Paine] stileing himself Historian ordered to lay on the Table. Committee appointed to conferr with a Committee of the Assembly and a Committee of the Execitive Council of the State of Pennsylvania, Reported that they had finishd the Conferrance, (Happily) and that they had 4 different charges against Major General Arnold, which the Commander in Chief is directed to have try'd by a Court Martial vizt. for an abuse in orderding the Shops of this City to be Shut, for sending a Malitia Sargant for a Barber for his Aid, for Employing the Public Waggons for Private use for [blank]

> Paine's letter was an attack on Congress for ruining his reputation by dismissing him

The Journal

from his post. The fourth charge against Arnold, which Fell omits, was granting permission for a ship owned by persons disaffected to the United States to come into port.

Sunday, April 4

Warm Rain.

Monday, April 5

Commercial Committee Congress. A Number of Letters Read. Clothier Generals Pay, the Report was 1000 Ds 12 Rations and forrege for 3 Horses. long debate carrd for 50000. State Clothier to be appointed & paid by the State. Commissary Turnbulls [Trumbull] affair came on but not finishd.

> The recommendation was for the Clothier-General to have a salary of $10,000, but Congress reduced it to $5,000. The settling of the late Commissary-General Joseph Trumbull's estate and accounts was still unfinished.

Tuesday, April 6

Commercial Committee Congress. Mr Rutgars [Rutgers] and Mr Horton appointed Deputy Muster Masters. Mr McPherson nominated. Order of the Day. Long Debate about Mr Dean [Deane] and the Commissioners abroad, on the Report of the Committee on foreign Affairs. P M Marine Committee.

Delegate from New Jersey

Wednesday, April 7

Commercial Committee. Congress. Sundry Letters Read. Motion for 15000 Ds. to be Paid to Captains, McNutt, Nevers, & Rogers, they are to endeavor to open a Road in to Novia Scotia. Order of the day, for examining in to the conduct of the Commissioners abroad, and foreign affairs, great and warm debates. agreed to Read all the Letters.

> From the beginning of the Revolution Alexander McNutt had endeavored to join Nova Scotia to the American cause. Nevers and Rogers were to open a road for easier communication with that province.

Thursday, April 8

Commercial Committee. Congress. Report from the Board of Warr to allow Barron Stiuben [von Steuben] 4000 Dolls Long Debate. Report of the Committee concerning the dispute abt prisoners between Major Pinkney [Pinckney] & Lt Coll Prevost agreed that Genl Lincoln should appoint a Commisary of Prisoners to the Southern Army. Marine Committee directed to Sell the Hulks of the Washington & Effingham Frigates. P.M. Marine Committee NB Dined with Mr Jay.

> The *Journals* do not record any discussion about Baron von Steuben.

Friday, April 9

Commercial Committee Congress. After the Let-

ters &c. The order of the Day In the Report of the Committee on foreign affairs. NB Dr Weatherspoon [Witherspoon] went home. P M. Marine Committee.

Saturday, April 10

Went to Mr Gills in Bucks County.

Sunday, April 11

At Mr Gills Very Hott,

Monday, April 12

Returnd to Town. Windy & Cold.

Tuesday, April 13

Commercial Committee. Congress. A Number of Letters, Reports of Committees, &c. &c. Report from the Treasury to be Printed P M Marine Committee

Wednesday, April 14

Commercial Committee Congress. Sundry Letters Read. On Motion for supplying the Officers with sundry articles at the price things were when they Enterd the Service & whether by the State they belong to, or by Congress long Debate.

Thursday, April 15

Commercial Committee Congress. Letter from Major Genl Lincoln March 7 by his Aid Major

Mead [Meade]. Letter from President Reed and the Resolves, relating to the Conferrence between the Congress and the Execitive Council & Assembly of the State of Pennsylvania to be Printed. Memorial from Sundry Surgeons and Doctors, Referrd to the Medical Committee. Letter from Lt Governor of Virginia Reccomending Coll Bland to be allowd a Table, Refer'd to the Delegates of the State. President Reed sent in a Letter from St Eustatia with an acct that Spain had acknowledgd the Independence of America. Report of the Board of Warr, Relating to the Regulating Waggons, Not determind Order of the Day for Consideration on foreign affairs, which occasion long Debates, and to very little purpose. Dr Wetherspoon [Witherspoon] at Congress. (Dined with Mr Lewis) P M Marine Committee.

> The controversy with Pennsylvania is central to the question of the relationship between Congress and the states. In this debate on foreign affairs, Congress was still trying to sort out the confusion of American ambassadors abroad.

Friday, April 16

Commercial Committee Congress. Letter from Major Genl Arnold relating to his being tryed by a Court Martial, Motion to lay on the Table Yas & Nas taken carried in the affirmitive. Treasury Report for 1000000 Ds. to Dr Potts, strongly op-

The Journal

posd all agreed there was great abuses in the Department Yas & Nas taken carried in the Negative, Motion for 800000 Yas & Nas. Negative. Motion then for 500000. Yas & Mas carried in the affirmitive. Report from the Committee of the Post Office Raised the price of Postage double and advanced the Sallerys of the different Officers. P M Marine Committee.

> Arnold was trying to speed up a decision. Dr. Potts was Deputy Director General of Military Hospitals for the Middle Department.

Saturday, April 17

Commercial Committee Congress. Long debate about the manner of Genl Lincolns leaving the Southern Army, on account of His Ill State of Health. Motion from the Delegates of Rhode Island to Raise 1500 men, long Debated &c. &c. Report from the Treasury for 50,000 Ds. in speicea to be sent to the Commissary General of Prisoners. Adjourned P M. M Committee on special Business. Dined with Mr Jay.

> No decision was made on the Rhode Island request.

Sunday, April 18

Last night very Cold and this morning thick Ice. Dined with Moses.

> This was probably Isaac Moses.

Delegate from New Jersey

Monday, April 19

Commercial Committee. Congress. Letter from Genl Green [Greene] reccomending many alterations in his department, Letter from S Deane Letter from Genl Irwin and other Prisoners Referd to the Board of Warr. Memorial with a Flag from Bermuda for Provision, committed to 3. Vizt. Ellery, Laurens and Fell. Letter from Major Genl Schuyler for leave to Resign his Commission, granted, and Reccomending Blankets to be sent to the Indians Referrd to the Bd of Warr. Report from the Board of Warr Reccomending when a Colonel is on Brigade Duty, that he be allowd 6 Rations extraordinary, agreed. Treasury Report for 1 Million for Coll Flowerss [Flower] department allowd 500,000 Motion for Rhode Island to Raise 1500 Men for a Year to be allowd the Cloathing &c. and £6 by Month and 200 Doll Bounty Ys & Ns carried in the Negative then 150 Ds Ys & Ns affirmitive 5 Ys 3 Ns 2 devided. Long Debate.

> Greene was Quartermaster-General. Flower was Commissary-General of Military Stores.

Tuesday, April 20

Coml Committee Congress. Letter from Govr Clinton, that the State of New York would Raise 1000 Men by Drafts from the Militia Order of the Day on foreign affairs, Very warm loud and long

The Journal

debate, relating to the Commissioners. lasted till 5 oClock. (Dr Wetherspoon [Witherspoon] gone home) P M Marine Committee

> The debate about the foreign ministers was indeed "warm loud and long." On the first two roll calls Fell voted, but since he was the only New Jersey delegate present, the state was not represented. On the final eight roll calls there is no vote recorded for any New Jersey delegate.

Wednesday, April 21

Commercal Committee Congress. Motion made by R H Lee & Seconded by Mr Carmichal [Carmichael], the doors of Congress should be open some very severe remarks on the impropriety of the motion, agree'd to Committ it to 5 vizt. Mr Lee Mr [Samuel] Adams Mr Lovell Mr Laurens & Mr Ellery. Letter from T. Payne [Paine] (lay on the Table) Order of the Day for foreign affairs, Report of the Committee that all the Commissioners be Recall'd amended by seperating the names, and that the Name of Dr B. Franklin Minister Plenopitentary be first put, long debate about his Carractor, till 4 oC and then adjournd

> There is no mention in the *Journals* about the discussion of Franklin.

Thursday, April 22

Commercial Comm Congress Letter from Genl

75

Delegate from New Jersey

Mullenburgh [Muhlenberg] about Rank Do [letter] from Colonels Van Courtland & Gansevoort abt Do [rank]. Referrd to the Board of Warr. Letter from Genl Washington. Do [letter] from Genl Green [Greene] in Town, Referrd to Whipple Morris & Armstrong. Judge McKean. Order of the Day on foreign affairs, after long debate till past. 4 the Question was put whether Dr Franklin should be Recall'd, Yas & Nas, card. in the Negative P M Marine Committee

> McKean was Chief Justice of Pennsylvania. Apparently, he attended this day.

Friday, April 23

Commercial Committee Congress. Mr S Adams moved that Mr McKean being Enterd on the Journals as attending, might be cancelld and a Debate insued agreed to stand. Letter from T Payne [Paine], and extract inclosed, Read. Letter from Capt Albouy Read, Committee Reported on the Petition from Bermuda for Provision, against granting the Yas & Nas being call'd & 5 for & 5 agst the Question was lost, Recommitted. Report from the Committee appointed to Conferr with General Green [Greene]. Rhode Island Motion for Raising 1500 Men long Debate (J. Dickenson [Dickinson] from DeLaware) P. M. Marine Committee

> The debate about McKean is not mentioned in the *Journals*. The committee to

consider the request for aid from the citizens of Bermuda reported that the island was guarded by British ships and garrisoned by British soldiers. Under these conditions aid would be difficult to provide, no matter how desirable, and thus should be denied. Since Fell was the only delegate from New Jersey voting, the state was not represented. If his yes vote had been counted the committee report would have been accepted. As it was it failed and was recommitted. General Nathaniel Greene reported that the Quartermaster's Department was deeply in debt and could not carry out the orders of General Washington without considerably more money. He also reported that morale was low in his department due to poor salaries and some actions he was required to take. Unless pay was increased many of his assistants would leave the service, and he would resign himself. The committee recommended money be made available for wagons and that salaries be considered soon. No action was taken at this time. The debate on the Rhode Island question revolved around the salaries to be paid the Rhode Island troops. After long debate and several votes, Congress agreed to consider accepting the new troops provided that they be paid no more than other Continental troops. Fell may not have remained for the long debate since he is not listed as voting on four roll calls. Dickinson took his seat in Congress.

Saturday, April 24

Commercial Committee Congress. Letter from the Claimants of the Sloop Active being Read after Debate, Motion to deferr the consideration to the 15th Sepr. The Assembly for the State of Pensylvania being to meet in August. Board of Warr Report that Ewing Commissary of Hides, have his Risignation accepted, and continue in office till another person be appointed, Reccomitted.
NB. Dr Benjn Franklin Minister Plenoptenary, first
Silas Deane.
Arthur Lee. Court of Madrid (Never has been there)
Ralph Izard Court of Tuscany . . . . No use
Willm Lee. Courts of Viena & Berlin . . No use
J. Adams. Private.

> The problem with the sloop *Active* is not explained. Consideration was delayed, however, until a committee could have time to confer with a committee of the General Assembly of Pennsylvania. George Ewing apparently wished to resign. The portion of the report of the Board of War regarding this request was recommitted. The list of names is appended to Fell's notes for this day, but nothing of this sort is mentioned in the *Journals*. This is apparently a list of American ambassadors with Fell's evaluations. The comment about John Adams is not clear.

Monday, April 26

Commercial Committee   Congress. A number of Letters Read &c. Order of the Day, Whether Mr Arthur Lee should be Recall'd, which occasiond very warm Debates indeed. continued till 5 oClock. P M Marine Committee, (Dr Wetherspoon [Witherspoon] & Dr Scudder)

> Arthur Lee was the minister to Spain, but he had never been there. The controversy with Silas Deane was still brewing, and the status of all the ministers was under consideration. Apparently Fell refers to a report of the Committee on Foreign Affairs which was considered at this time. Both Witherspoon and Scudder returned to Congress.

Tuesday, April 27

Coml Committee   Congress. Petition from General Arnold   Letters from S. Deane. Genl Gates   Genl Heath, General Washington, order on the Treasury for 2000 Guineas   Letter from Lt Hale [Hele], Committed Auditors 8 Ds by Day. Jos Howell nominated   This day, too much like many others, spent in Debate to answer no valuable purpose. P M. Marine Committee

> Congress authorized 2,000 guineas for General Washington for use in secret services. This action was recorded in the Manuscript Secret Journal, not the regular *Journals*.

Delegate from New Jersey

The Board of Treasury recommended an additional auditor for the army and suggested Captain Joseph Howell. The Board also recommended that salaries for auditors be raised to $8.00 per day. All these proposals were approved.

Wednesday, April 28

Coml Committee Congress Letter from Bermuda for Indian Corn, Refd to the same Committee as the last. Memorial from General Green [Greene] on behalf of himself & Deputys Referrd to the Committed appointed to Confer with G Green [Greene] Memorial of the Sloop Active. This Sloop gives a great deal of trouble, committed to the 15 Sepr. Letter from General Arnold, relating to papers to be furnished him for his Tryall. A Letter from Govr Reed, complaining exceedingly of Congress with Respect to their Ill useage as a State, and neglect shewn them in a particular manner, and the Old affair of Genl Arnold Renewd a very serious Letter indeed. Motion to Committ it to the same Committee who held the Conferrence with the Committee of Council and Assembly before. P M Commercial Committee met by order to consult abt purchasing a Cargoe of Goods from France NB One Invoice 45 & another 60 for 1 advance.

Concerning the letters from Bermuda and Greene, see entry for April 23. The request was from claimants of the *Active* who asked that their claims be paid in advance; the money would be returned with interest if Congress decided against them. No action was taken at this time. See entry for April 24. The comments about invoices are not clear.

Thursday, April 29

Coml Committee. Congress. The chief of this day spent in consideration on the Subject of Finance, and to Tax largely. P M. Thunder, Lightening, Hail and Rain Went to Marine Committee No Members.

> The bulk of the day was spent on discussion of raising supplies and supporting the Continental currency. No votes were taken.

Friday, April 30

Commercial Committee Congress. Order of the day, on the Report of the Committee on foreign affairs, Motion for Recalling Mr Arthur Lee on which Mr Paca and Mr Drayton moved for a paper being Read and Enter'd, containing a Conferrence with Mr Gerrard [Gerard], concerning Mr Lees Conduct at the Court of France & Spain, Objection being made caused long & warm debate, on both sides, I moved for an amendment instead of Recalling Mr Lee, to have his Commission Vacated, debate lasted, till near 5 oClock. P M Marine Committee.

Arthur Lee, American ambassador to the Court of Madrid, was under consideration. Congressmen Paca and Drayton reported that he was unacceptable to the Courts of Madrid and Versailles. They reported that Gerard, Minister Plenipotentiary from France, and Count de Vergennes, Foreign Minister of France, were very distrustful of him. Under such circumstances, they believed Lee would not be able to represent the United States in peace negotiations that might begin at any time. They therefore asked for his recall. Fell's motion is not recorded in the *Journals*.

Saturday, May 1

Commercial Committee Congress. This day intirely spent in debate, concerning Mr A Lee.

> There were other matters also under consideration, but the bulk of the time was spent on the recall of Arthur Lee.

Sunday, May 2

Dined with Mr. Steward.

Monday, May 3

Commercial Committee Congress. The Business of this day intirely taken up till 5 oClock on the Question of Recalling Mr A Lee 4 Yeas 4 Noes 4 States Divided, (Dined wth President Reed[ )] NB For his Recall 22 Yeas. Nays 14. R. H. Lee Excused Mr. Plater absent, & Mr McKean

The Journal

Other items of business preceded the vote on Arthur Lee. Fell voted to recall him but was outvoted in New Jersey by Witherspoon and Scudder. The result was an equal division of the states. Fell apparently noted the total individual votes to show that a majority of the delegates favored recall but were so scattered among the states that they could not prevail. R. H. Lee was excused from voting because he was related to Arthur Lee. Fell may have mentioned the absence of Plater and McKean because he believed their votes would have allowed a decision to be made.

Tuesday, May 4

Commercial Committee Congress. Letter from the King of France, sent by Mr Jarrard [Gerard] acquainting Congress, with the Birth of a Princess. A Committee of one Member from Each State appointed to wait on the Minister in consequence, and a Committee of three to write a Letter to the King in answer. A Number of Letters and Memorials, Read, The request from Rhode Island to Raise Men for one Year, granted P M. Marine Committee.

> Rhode Island had requested permission to raise 1,500 men for one year's service. Congress agreed, subject to the provision that they not be paid more than other Continental troops. See entry for April 23. Fell voted no on the request.

Delegate from New Jersey

Wednesday, May 5

Commercial Committee Congress. Report from the Treasury, relating to the setling the late Commissary General Trunbulls [Trumbull] accts. long debate, at last agree'd his Brother be impowerd to setle them. Agreea'd that the Troops Raising in Virginia and North Carolina, with Blands & Bailors [Baylor] Dragoons, be sent for the deffence of Georgia & So Carolina Committee to whom was Refferd the Petition of the Inhabitants of Bermuda, Reported for Indian Corn to be sent them, (not determined on), Motion to ajour to 5 oClock, to morrow being fast Day, carried in the Negative

> The settlement of Trumbull's accounts was finally arranged. The matter of Bland and Baylor is entered in the *Journals* for May 7. See entry for that date.

Thursday, May 6

Fast Day.

> Congress did not meet on this day.

Friday, May 7

Commercial Committee. Congress. A Number of Letters and Memorials & another Petition from Bermuda, for Bread, after long debate agreed to Rejct their Petition alltogether. Letter from General Washington enclosing Letters from General

The Journal

Schuyler, that some of the Six Nations were suing for Peace, and that intelegence from Canada was 1500 Regulars and some Canadians were expected on the Frontiers &c. Letter from Mr Jarrard [Gerard] that by his last Accounts England expected to act vigorosly & determind to push the Warr. P M Marine Committee.

> The committee considering the request from Bermuda recommended that Pennsylvania, Delaware, Maryland, Virginia, and North Carolina each allow 1,000 bushels of Indian corn to be sent for the relief of the residents of the island. However, a substitute motion to provide no aid was adopted. Fell voted against the substitute. According to the *Journals* Congress took action on this day concerning troops for the South and not on May 5 as indicated in Fell's diary. Both Virginia and North Carolina had not filled their quotas for defense of the South. Congress now requested that light dragoons under Colonel Bland and Colonel Baylor be sent immediately to reinforce the Southern army and that the two states be requested to fill their quotas as soon as possible.

Saturday, May 8

Commercial Committee Congress. Order of the Day on foreign affairs. Question whether a shair of the Fishery on the Banks of Newfoundland should be an Ultimatom in case our Allies should

Delegate from New Jersey

agree to terms with Great Britain, Long Debate. Letter from Mr Gerrard [Gerard] Presing the necesity of fixing on a Proper Person to be appointed Minister Plenoptentary to the Court of Madrid.

> The question of the fishing grounds was a vexing one. A proposal was made that under any treaty the right of fishing on the coasts and banks of North America be reserved to the United States as fully as when they were colonies. An attempted substitute to delete the fisheries question was voted down as out of order. No final action was taken.

Monday, May 10

Commercial Committee Congress. This day a Letter was Read from Governor Levingston [Livingston], and also the Memorials of the Officers of the State of New Jersey. Letter from Genl Washington with an acct of Coll VanScacks [Van Schaick] Expedition to the Onendagos [Onondaga] also an acct of the Imbarkation of 8 Regiments from N York and the Conferrence with the Commissioners for the Excha of Prisoners at Amboy, orderd to be Printed. Letter from the Minister, reccomending the finishing the appointment of a Minister to Spain. &c. &c. Expidition reccomended to Genl Washington. A Letter from Mr DeFranca [de Francy] and a long Memorial from Mr Biau-

The Journal

marsha [Beaumarchais] (not finish'd). Count DeEstang [d'Estaing]

Due to the press of other urgent business, Congress delayed action on the New Jersey request with a promise to consider it as soon as possible. Apparently the letters concerned army matters. While serving under General James Clinton, Colonel Goose Van Schaick led a force of 500 men from Fort Schuyler into the country of the Onondaga Indians, where he burned their principal settlement, destroyed provisions and cattle, took thirty-two prisoners, and killed a number of Indians. This was accomplished in six days without a casualty. Congress voted its thanks to the colonel and his command for the action. The actions of Colonels Davies and Harrison in attempting to exchange prisoners with the British was approved by Congress, which issued a statement to the American prisoners "to persevere in enduring their captivity with the magnanimity and patience by which they have hitherto been distinguished . . ." and to be assured that Congress was attempting to get them released by every means possible. A letter from M. de Francy along with a memorial concerning the payment of debts to M. de Beaumarchais was read in part. Further consideration was delayed until the next day. Fell's reference to d'Estaing is unclear in purpose.

Tuesday, May 11

Commercial Committee Congress. Mr Franceys [de Francy] Memorial Relating to Mr Beamarsha [Beaumarchais] Read after some debate agreed to a Committee of five to consider and Report thereon vizt. Laurens, Smith Carmichael, Dickinson, Searle. Letter from Genl DePortail [du Portail] Respecting West Point. &c. Report from the Board of Warr respecting Enginears Genl DePortail [du Portail] appointed Commandant of the whole, A number of other Reports and appointments, in different departments read and agreed to, the Minister of France told the President, if Congress would write to the King, for the purpose, he would send clothing &c. for the Army to be paid for after a Peace. A Noble generous Offer P M Marine Committee

> Mr. de Francy was the agent of Beaumarchais. He was still trying to get payment from Congress for the goods acquired from France by Silas Deane. Congress resolved that engineers, sappers (builders of trenches and fortifications), and miners (those who dig and lay mines) be paid the same as men of the same rank in the artillery. General du Portail was appointed commander of the corps of engineers and companies of sappers and miners. As a result of the offer from France, Congress ordered the Marine Committee and the Board of War to draw up a list of articles needed.

Wednesday, May 12

Coml Committee Congress. Letter from Mr Bingham at Martinica [Martinique], Letter from the first Lievt of the Dean Frigate, proposing a plan to goe to the Island of St. Johns, Referrd to the Marine Committee to take order thereon. Order of the Day on the utlimatom of the Fishery. Long debate and several amendments propos'd.

> William Bingham, American agent in the West Indies, made regular reports. This one concerned the activities of the Count d'Estaing. Apparently, the letter from the *Dean* was from Pierre Dereville. The question on the ultimatum was whether the United States should demand fishing rights as a part of the treaty of peace and what the attitude of the allies would be. No decision was made.

Thursday, May 13

Commercial Committee Congress, This day spent in very triffling debate P M Marine Committee.

> This included Treasury reports, payment of accounts, reports from the Board of War about promotion, and more debate on the fishery question.

Friday, May 14

Congress. Letter from Govr. Johnson of MaryLand advising Mr Hollinshead [Hollingsworth] at the

Delegate from New Jersey

Head of Ellk of a Fleet of between 30 & 40 Sail being in Chesapeek Bay. Mr Smith introduced a paper of Rivingston [Rivington] of the 5th. with a Letter said to be wrote by Mr Laurens to the Governor of Georgia. Long debate whether in order or No Yaes & Nayes carried in the Negative. P M Marine Comm

> Congress referred the matter reported by Governor Johnson to the Board of War to take necessary action to prevent an enemy invasion of Chesapeake Bay and to prevent stores from falling into his hands. Meriwether Smith introduced a newspaper, printed by James Rivington, which included a letter from Henry Laurens to Governor Houstoun of Georgia. Smith claimed the letter to be derogatory, injurious, and dangerous to the confidence in Congress. He asked that the letter be read and Laurens called on to acknowledge his authorship. Long debate ensued concerning whether Smith's actions were in order. The action was declared out of order; Fell voted that it was not in order.

Saturday, May 15

Went to Bristol.

> Fell did not attend Congress this day. However, the question concerning the Laurens letter continued. Laurens addressed the House to explain his contempt for Smith's action. In order, he said, to

avoid questions about his character, he admitted writing a private letter to Governor Houstoun which he would produce upon request of Congress. The request was not made.

Sunday, May 16

went to Mr Gills

Monday, May 17

A M came to Town Congress. A number of Letters Memorials &c. from Genl Washington, Genl Lincoln, Genl Maxwell Coll Morgan, Dallaware [Delaware] Indians. &c. &c.

Tuesday, May 18

Com. Committee Congress. Several Letters, Petitions &c. Read. Report of the Committee to whom was Referrd the Memorial from Bermuda, agreed to let them have Indian Corn not Exceeding 1000 Bushel. P M. Went to Marine Committee (did not make a Board[ )]

> The committee to consider the Bermuda request for aid asked that the matter be reconsidered since intelligence indicated that the suffering was real and that the supplies would be well used. The resolution asked Pennsylvania, Delaware, Maryland, Virginia, and North Carolina each to allow 1,000 bushels of Indian corn to be shipped on the understanding that a certifi-

cate would be returned to each executive officer certifying delivery and proper use. After an attempt to remove North Carolina from the resolution failed, the recommendation for aid passed. Fell and Scudder of New Jersey voted for the measure.

Wednesday, May 19

Commercial Committee Congress. After reading the Letters, The order of the day of Finance, after long debate; the Question was put for filling the Blank in the 4 article, with 60 Million of Dolls. carried in the Negative then the question for 45 Million, carried in the affirmitive. 5 Yaes 4 Noes — 2 divided. NB. Dr Wetherspoon [Witherspoon] at Congress.

> Previously Congress had left blank the amount to be collected from the states by January 1, 1780. This was an attempt to set the amount. The first attempt to raise $60 million failed by a vote of 7 to 2 with two states divided. The second figure of $45 million passed. Fell voted no on the $60 million and yes on the $45 million.

Thursday, May 20

Commercial Committee Congress. Letter from Seiur Gerrard [Gerard], relating to 2 Spanish Vessells carried in to the State of Massachusets Bay. Referrd to a Committee of three vizt. Mr Smith of Virginia read and presented a Resolve of their Assembly, relating to the Confederation. Order of the day on foreign affairs   Whether Mr Izard should be Recall'd, from the Court of Tuscany. Debate whether he should be recall'd, or his Commission Vacated, no determination   Adjournd to 10 oClock. NB A Letter was read from Leesburgh in Virginia that the Enemy had Landed there, that Major [blank] had defended Fort with 150 Men, till he was oblidg'd to leave it that he Spiked up the Guns, destroyd all the Stores, Burnt 3 Ships on the Stocks, and that a party of 30 were sent of which he Killed 14 and took 16 Prisoners.

> Gerard's letter was concerned about three Spanish ships taken by privateers and carried into Massachusetts. Smith's statement concerned Maryland's refusal to ratify the Articles of Confederation until the states, especially Virginia, gave up their claims on western lands. Virginia proposed here that a partial confederation be created of all states willing to join. This was an obvious attempt to get around Maryland's obstacle and still allow Virginia to retain its western claims. This resolution from Virginia gave her delegates the authority to enter such a partial confederation. Ralph Izard was never received by the Court of Tuscany, to which he had been appointed in 1777. He remained in Paris, where he came into conflict with Benjamin Franklin. These were the primary reasons for considering his recall. The name Fell omits in the Virginia battle was Mathews.

Friday, May 21

Commercial Committee   Congress. Letter from the Legislature of N Jersey for an explination of some Resolves of Congress. Referrd to the Board of Warr. Letter from Genl Thompson & Coll Webb in behalf of themselves, Genl Waterberry [Waterbury], Cols Honsecker, Pottor [Potter] & Alison, to let Gens Philips [Phillips] Esdale & their aids go to New York on Parole, Committed to 3 vizt. Spencer Atley [Atlee] & Scudder. Order of the Day on Finance Agreed to Levy 45 Million of Dollars by Tax this Year in addition to 15 do [million] allready orderd to be Raisd. Motion from Dickinson to have a Spireted Adress sent to the people at large shewing the Necesity of the measure, Committee to draw it up viz Dickinson Drayton & Lee. Letter from Govr Henry of Virginia dated 12th Instt with an acct of the Enemy being at Portsmouth. Petition of Dodge & Wood, who have been Prisoners a Detroit. NB Dr Weatherspoon [Witherspoon] gon home NB the Gentlemen sent with the Letter from New Jersey Mr Elijah Clark [Clarke] & Silas Conduit [Condict] P M. Went to Marine Committee did not make a Bd.

> Congress directed that New Jersey be given the information requested. In considering taxation, an attempt to change the date of payment from January to April 1780 failed. This was the completion of the action taken on May 19.

The Journal

Saturday, May 22

Commercial Committee Congress. Several Letters Read, and an affadavit of particulers relating to the Cruelty of the Enemy in Virginia &c. Memorial from the State of New York relating to the seperation of the State of Vermont postponed the consideration till next Saturday, The order of the day on foreign affairs, deferrd till Tuesday on account of a Long letter from the Seiur Gerrard [Gerard].

> According to the New York report, the territory of Vermont was jointly controlled during the colonial period by New York and New Hampshire. Now Vermont was attempting to become a separate state. The New York resolution was designed to prevent such action.

Sunday, May 23

Fine Weather.

Monday, May 24

Com Committee Congress. A very long letter, from Mr Deane & a great deal of Debate, to very little purpose and very little Business done.

Tuesday, May 25

Com Committee. Congress. Mr. Dickinson one of the Committee to bring in a draft of a Letter to adress the People, and Read the same and the day

Delegate from New Jersey

taken up on the same. NB. Did not attend the Marine Committee.

Wednesday, May 26

Commercial Committee   Congress. A Letter from T Payne [Paine], abusing Mr Deane was Read and took up a deal of time in debate. The Adress to the People was read paragraph by paragraph and unanimously agreed to and 500 Copies orderd to be printed. One of the Delegates of the State of Pennsylvania informd the House that the President with some other Gentlemen, were at the door, waiting with a Petition which they would be glad to Represent, in such way as would be most agreeable, after some short time, it was agreed, that the Secretary should desire the President and the Gentlemen with him to come in and present the Petition, which he did and after a short Introductory Speech on the Occasion, the Gentlemen withdrew, and Petition was Read.

> Paine's letter was a continuation of the controversy between Silas Deane and Arthur Lee concerning the French loans. Paine, writing under the pen name "Common Sense," was a supporter of Lee. The thrust of the address to the people was to encourage the public to support the war, especially in a financial way. The *Journal* entry notes that the petition from Pennsylvania was "relative to the subject of Finance," but this statement was later

crossed out. Since the President of Pennsylvania was concerned that some members felt his petition was improper, Congress unanimously resolved that sentiments of the public dealing with important matters would always be received cheerfully.

Thursday, May 27

Commercial Committee Congress. Letter from the Sieur Girrard [Gerard] was Read The order of the day, for taking up the Ultimatom on the fishery, after many speaches and long debates, it was agreed to withdraw and Repeal all the former, Resolutions amendments and Subsitutes, and begin anew.

> Congress did agree that no treaty should give up the right of a common fishery.

Friday, May 28

Commercial Committee Congress. Letter from Genl Washington abt So Carolina Order of the Day, on Fineance, some consideration on Do. [finance] P M Marine Committee. Mrs Fell & Peter sent for

Saturday, May 29

Com. Committee Congress. Letter from So Carolina, Order of the day to taken in to consideration, the dispute between the States of New York and Vermont.

No final settlement was reached and the issue was continued to June 1.

Monday, May 31

Com. Committee, did not goe to Congress

Tuesday, June 1

Commercial Committee Congress. Order of the day to consider the matter relating to New York and Vermont.

> Congress agreed to appoint a committee to look into the dispute concerning Vermont. The committee was to promote an amiable settlement provided that the rights of the states were maintained and that justice was provided to the citizens in both states.

Wednesday, June 2

Com Committee Congress. This day chiefly spent on Finance.

Thursday, June 3

Coml Committee Congress. After the Letters were Read, The Order of the day relating to the ultimatom on the Fishery

> This was a further attempt to protect American fishing rights in any treaty that might be arranged. No final decision was reached.

The Journal

Friday, June 4

Did not goe to Congress this day.

Saturday, June 5

Coml Committee   Congress. A Number of Letters from Genl Washington advising of the Enemy being in great force gon up the No River, suppos'd to Wt. Point Fort

Sunday, June 6

Dined at Mr Greys

Monday, June 7

Commercial Committee   Congress. Sundry Letters, and long debates abt Coll Wadsworth, Commissary Generals Resigning.

> J. Wadsworth, Commissary General of Purchases, offered to resign because of alleged irregularities in his department. Congress voiced its confidence in him and refused to accept the resignation because of the danger and confusion it would create.

Tuesday, June 8

Com. Committee   Congress. Order of the Day of the Report of Recalling Mr Izard. 7 Ayes 4 Noes 1 divided. Willm Lee 7 do [Ayes] 4 do [Noes] 1 do [divided].

> On the recall of Izard, New Jersey was the one state divided. Fell voted yes and

99

Scudder no. William Lee was appointed in 1777 as commissioner to the courts of Berlin and Vienna, but neither country was disposed toward recognition of the United States. Through two years of activity William Lee was not able to make any headway. During this period he did become heavily involved in the Silas Deane-Arthur Lee controversy. New Jersey was again the divided state, with Scudder and Fell voting the same as on Mr. Izard.

Wednesday, June 9

Com. Committee Congress. After reading the Letters, the Order of the Day on Finance, was taken up, and several proposal Read, all which were agreed to be left to a Committee of 6 to Report on Friday.

Thursday, June 10

C Committee Congress, Order of the Day on the Committee of 13 long debates concerning the detaining S Deane and Recalling Arthur Lee &c.
  No decision was reached.

Friday, June 11

Coml. Committee Congress. Order of the Day on finance agreed to borrow on Loan 20,000,000 to be paid in 3 Year or when the Money is $1/8$ better than at presant

The Journal

The deadline for receiving the money was October 1. The loan would pay interest of six percent.

Saturday, June 12

Com. Committee   NB. Did not goe to Congress. Dr. Morgons [Morgan] affair decided   P M. Commercial Committee

> Dr. John Morgan had been Director General and Physician in Chief in the general hospitals of the United States until his removal on January 9, 1777, because of complaints from the army and the critical state of affairs. After Morgan requested an inquiry into his conduct, Congress appointed an investigating committee on September 18, 1778. Its report, adopted by Congress, exonerated Dr. Morgan of any wrongdoing and commended him for his service.

Sunday, June 13

A M. Went to Committee, to dispatch The Eagle Packet   Capt Ashmead to Martinique.

Monday, June 14

Com. Committee   Congres. After the dispatches were read the order of the Day on Finance, long debated for increasing the Interest.

Written in the margin for this date were the following figures:

1/8	260 000	1 00000
	32 500	50000
	227 50/0	25000
	11375	12500
	4375	4375
	15750	

This obviously concerns the interest on the loan, but the exact meaning is unclear.

Tuesday, June 15

Coml Committee Congress. Sundry Letters and Reports from Committees, a Memorial from Mr Horton one of the Muster Masters, in behalf of himself and the rest Referrd to a Committee of 3 Vizt. [blank] P M. Marine Committee.

> The committee appointed consisted of Henry Laurens, Joseph Spencer, and Nathaniel Scudder.

Wednesday, June 16

Com. Committee Congres Letter from Genl Washington, relating to the Enemys movements at the North River. Report from the Committee appointed to the affair of Vermont & N York, after debate agreed to. Order of the Day on finance, Motion for raising the Interest to former

The Journal

lenders, to make good the Loss on deppriciation. Long Debate 9 A M. S F & Peter sett off

> This report concerned relations between New York and New Hampshire. A decision on the issue of Vermont was delayed until the committee agreed to on June 1 reported. S. F. and Peter were Fell's wife and son. They returned to New Jersey after a short visit to Philadelphia.

Thursday, June 17

Commercial Committee Congress. After the Dispatches &c. were Read, the Order of the Day on fixing the Ultimatom for Instructions to the Minister Plenopentiary &c. P M. 6. oClock Marine Committee

> No action was taken on the ultimatum.

Friday, June 18

Com. Committee Congress. Sundry dispatches Memorials &c. A Memorial from Cs. Pettit D Q G complaining of the State of New Jersey Taxing him and Mr Cox from one to ten thousand pound at the discretion of the Assesor. Committed to 3 vizt. Mr McKean Mr Paca Mr Lovell. Order of the day on finance long debate whether the lenders on former Loans from March 1st 1778 should have the promise of their Interest being put on the same footing as those, are, which are to have an increase of Interest on the present Loan if the money should farther depriciate. Duane, Scudder, Paca, Henry, Smith, Fleming, Burk [Burke], Laurens, Drayton No. P M Marine Committee.

> This was an attempt to raise the interest on former loans so that lenders would not suffer due to a depreciation of Continental currency. Fell voted yes. Just why he included this list of names is not clear. They voted no on the issue, but so did Jenifer of Maryland. The motion passed, 7-3, with two states, including New Jersey, divided.

Saturday, June 19

Commercial Committee. Congress. After the Letter &c. The order of the day on the Report of the Committee on the Memorial from Mr Girrard [Gerard], after some debate to very little purpose, the Eastern Members made a new motion about the Fishery, to which amendments were propos'd and long and Idle debates ensued according to custom, when ever the fishery is the subject.

> This concerned the possible treaty with Great Britain, American positions as concerned the French, and the continuing question of the fisheries.

Monday, June 21

Com Committee Congress Order of the Day on finance, long debate, and nothing done.

The Journal

Tuesday, June 22

Com Committee. Congress, This wholy taken up in Reading Letters Memorials and Petitions &c. Motion for appointing a Clothier General, Mr Wickoff was nominated by Genl Armstrong and Mr Scudder, Peter R Fell was nominated by Mr Duane. Deferr'd till Thursday P M Marine Committee.

Wednesday, June 23

Coml Committee Congress. Sundry Letters and Reports Read. A Memorial from the Legislature of New Jersey was read, relating to the appointment of Officers Referrd to a Committee of 3 vizt. Sherman, Morris and Scudder. Order of the Day on Finance One the Question for Mr Dickinsons amendment for the Interest to be secur'd to the lender of the present Loan and to have Retrospect to goe back to 1st March 1778 6 Yaes. 4 Noes 2 States divided. On the Main Question Mr Scudder call'd for the Yaes & Naes and said his Life might deppend on his Vote being known, All Yaes except, Scudder Duane & Paca

> Congress was still considering the problem of guaranteeing the value of money in face of its continuing depreciation. What Scudder's comment means is unclear.

Thursday, June 24

Coml Committee Congress. When the Letters &c. were read. The Order of the day for the taking up the Ultimatom for the fishery, and after a number of amendments, the Question was put and carried in the affirmitive as follows viz Yaes 5 Noes 4. Divided 3 of which N Jersey was one, I was no, under a full conviction, notwithstanding the importance of the fishery that these United States are not equal to continue the Warr without the assistance of our ally, provided we could have an honorable Peace, without insisting on this claim purely to serve the Eastern States. Peter Wickoff appointed Clothier General

> This vexing fishery question bothered Fell a great deal. He hoped that this ended the discussion although he was outvoted on the question. No mention is made in the *Journals* about why Peter Fell was not elected Clothier-General.

Friday, June 25

Coml Committee Congress. After the dispatches, the Order of the Day on finance, chiefly relating to the mode of the Certificates for the New Loan, the Treasury report to have them paid to the holder, his Heirs Executors and administrators to prevent their being Negotiated. long debated, nothing done. Exceeding hott, in the Evening, Thunder, Lightening and hard Rain.

> There was great concern that certificates might become speculative instruments. This was an attempt to prevent such use.

The Journal

Saturday, June 26

Coml Committee Congress. This day spent in Reading Letters, Petitions, Memorials & Reports from the Treasury Board and Board of War &c.

Monday, June 28

Commercial Committee Congress, This day spent in Reading Letters Reports from Committees &c. President [John Jay] Sick.

Tuesday, June 29

Coml Committee Congress. Severall dispatches and Reports from Committes, a Question put by the Secreatary whether Coll Ethan Allen should be supply'd with Copys of Papers relating to him &c. debate on the propriety of granting them, (agreed he should [)] P M Marine committee, orderd a Brig to be Built.

> The Allen matter is not mentioned in the *Journals*.

Wednesday, June 30

Coml Committee Congress. After the Letters and reports from Committees, the Order of the day on finance was taken up and some Resolves relating to the Loan for 20 Million of Dolls. agreed to and ordered to be printed.

Thursday, July 1

Coml Committee. Congress. A number of Letters Read, and one from Major Genl Green

[Greene] Quarter Master General of a very insolant nature indeed highly Reflecting on the Legislature for having Taxed two of his assistants Coll Cox and Coll Petit [Pettit], and thretening to Re ign &c. After speaking on the subject, and to treat it as I thought it deservd, I moved to have it lie on the Table, but that motion was over ruled and it was Committed to McKean Duane & Burk [Burke]. after the order of the Day, Debates on the Fishery &c. Marine Committee.

> The *Journals* make only a terse entry that the letter from Greene was received and committed. Although Fell hoped the question of the fishery had been settled (see note for June 24), it obviously had not been.

Friday, July 2

C. Committee Congress. Sundry Letters Petitions &c. were read Order of the Day on finance agreed to sundry Resolves relating to the extending the time for Receiving the Emissions of April & May call'd out of Circulation.

> This was an attempt to take out of circulation Continental currency that had depreciated in value. The delay was allowed because of the fighting and general confusion in several states.

The Journal

Saturday, July 3

Coml Committee Congress. Letters Memorials, Reports from the Treasury Board &c. This days Paper was read wherein a Letter sign'd Leonidas was introduced, and a motion made by Mr Gerry to send for the Printer, to know the author, long debate and the privious question being calld for and carried in the Affirmitive, the Motion drop'd.

> There is no debate recorded in the *Journals* on the letter.

Sunday, July 4

this being the Annaversaire of our Indipendence, the Chaplains of Congress were orderd to prepare Sermons suitable for the Ocasion.

> The action of Congress to prepare a celebration occurred on June 24. Interestingly enough, both New Jersey delegates, Fell and Scudder, voted against a celebration.

Monday, July 5

Coml Committee Congress Adjournd at 12 oClock to hear Mr Braunridges [Brackenridge] Elogium on the Heroes Slain in this Contest. Afterwards there was an Entertainment at the City Tavern. And in the Evening Currious fire works.

> None of this is mentioned in the *Journals*.

Tuesday, July 6

Commercial Committee Congress. Several Letters Read, Afterwards the Order of the Day, relating to the Fishery, after debating in the Old track till near 4 oClock Adjournd

Wednesday, July 7

Coml Committee   Congress   Letters from Mr Gerrard [Gerard] & Mr Holker referrd to a Committee, Searle Scudder & Lewis Order of the day on finance Agreed to Commissioner be appointed for the Treasury Board, and to sundry other regulations in that department.

Thursday, July 8

Coml Committee   Congress   Sundry Letters from Major G Lincoln   Genl Moultre [Moultrie] & Govr Rutledge, Referrd to a Committee. Letter and offer to Resign from Coll Cox & Coll Petitt [Pettit], also Referrd to a Committee, Report for fixing Sundry Prizes for the army, to be considered on Saturday

> These letters from Lincoln, Moultrie, and Rutledge were concerned with military defense in South Carolina and Georgia. The Assembly of New Jersey enacted a tax on officials of the United States Government. General Nathaniel Greene, Quartermaster-General, had protested to Congress several times. Cox and Pettit, Assistant Quartermasters-General, were particularly distressed. A report of the committee considered the New Jersey act discriminatory and asked that it be repealed. Congress

The Journal

also resolved that the officials continue in their duties until a final disposition of the matter could be made.

Friday, July 9

Commercial Committee   Congress. This day was spent on a Report, relating to the Quarter Master and Commisary departments &c. Mr Wm C. Houston, a delegate from New Jersey, took his Seat in Congress to day.

> These actions were attempts to prevent fraud and dishonesty in two very important departments that had large financial responsibility. Houston's arrival raised the New Jersey delegation to four. The others were Fell, Scudder, and Witherspoon. Houston's credentials stated that New Jersey expected at least three delegates to be in regular attendance.

Saturday, July 10

Coml Committee   Congress. Letters Memorials and Reports from the Board of War and Treasury, Letter from Peter Wickof [Wikoff] to Resign the appointment of Clothier General and several other persons put in Nomination. Dr Wetherspoon [Witherspoon] attended Congress to day.

> Wikoff declined to accept the office. Others nominated were James Stevenson, Samuel Caldwell, George Measom, and William Henry. The names of Caldwell and Henry

were later scratched from the *Journal* entry. On July 15 Congress proceeded to elect Perzifor Frazer to the office. Why Peter Fell was not put into nomination again is not clear.

Monday, July 12

After the dispatches at 12 oClock, Congress went in to a Committee of the whole to have a Conferrence with Mr Gerrard [Gerard]. Mr Lawrence [Laurens] was appointed Chairman and Mr Dickinson and Dr Wetherspoon [Witherspoon] assistance in the Conferrance, after the Minister was gon the Chairman obtained a writing [blank] which was Read, and desired leave to sitt againe President took the Chair and sundry Reports were read from the Board of War and Treasury.

> Laurens reported that the Committee of the Whole was not prepared to report the substance of the conference with the French minister. He asked permission to meet again and this was agreed to for the next day. This action was recorded only in the Manuscript Secret Journal, Foreign Affairs.

Tuesday, July 13

Coml Committee Congress Letter from Genl Washington dated Head Quarters New Windsor, July 9th. Committed to 3 viz. Mr Marchant [blank] [blank] Congress went in to a Committee

The Journal

of the whole on the subject of the Conferrence, the Chairman desird leave to sitt againe, and the President Resumed the Chair, and the Report of Duartee [Duarti], the Portugese was taken up and debated till past 4 oClock.

> Two blank spaces were left in Fell's diary. The two other members of the committee were Huntington and Armstrong. No mention is made of the Committee of the Whole in the *Journals*. Its meeting was only noted in the Secret Journal. No mention is made of the action regarding Duarti in the *Journals* for this date.

Wednesday, July 14

Coml Committee Congress. After the Letters &c were read, Went in to a Committee of the whole house, on the Conferrence with Mr Gerrard [Gerard], which the Chairman having Reduced to writing, Read in his place and after some time the President Resumed the Chair; Some foreign Letters were read. Dined with Mr Jay

> This was the report of the conference with the French minister. The long report discussed negotiations with Great Britain and the problems and potentials of a possible peace treaty.

Thursday, July 15

Commercial Committee Congress. Letters from some of the Commissioners in france were read wherein they advise of the English Ministry giving Orders to their Army here to Land at Wethersfield and burn and distroy all in their way to New Haven and there imbarque Letter from Mr Shearman [Sherman] mentions the Enemy having Burnt Fairfield, the whole Town except the Church. A Clothier General was appointed by Ballot. Coll [blank]

> The letters from France are not mentioned in the *Journals*. The new Clothier-General was Perzifor Frazer.

Friday, July 16

Com Committee Congress. This day almost intirely taken up in Reading A Lees Letters and Reflections againt S Deane did not adjourn till past 5 oClock. Dined with Mr Jay

> This is a continuation of the Deane-Lee dispute. Congress decided to seal all relevant papers until it could fully deal with the matter.

Saturday, July 17

Congress. Letter from Capt Cuningham [Conyngham] to his Wife acquainting her of his cruel treatment, Referrd to a Committee who Reported that a Letter be imideately wrote by the Secretary and sent to the Commanding Officer at New York to know where and in what manner Capt Cunningham [Conyngham] was treated &c. Order of the

Day on the Fisherie, according to Custom little done. Mr Dickinson read in his place what he would have adopted by way of Instructions to the Plenoptentary that may be sent to Negotiate for Peace. Report from the Bd of Warr Relating to Coll Malcolm; to be Reconsiderd

> Captain Conyngham was held prisoner by the British, but his wife feared that he was to be sent to England. A strong letter was sent to British commanders in New York with the stipulation that unless satisfaction were achieved by August 1, British prisoners would be held to correspond to Conyngham. No final action was taken on the fishery question.

Monday, July 19

Commercial Committee Congress A number of Letters and dispatches read Genl Waynes with an account of his having surprisd and taken the Garison at Stoney Point with 500 Men Genl Washington Letter with an acct of the Enemy having Plunderd New Haven and Burnt Fairfield Green Farms, Norwalk & Bedford &c. P M. Marine Committee.

> On this date Congress was informed that Perzifor Frazer had declined the office of Clothier-General because of the salary. New nominees were James Wilkinson and Peter Fell.

Delegate from New Jersey

Tuesday, July 20

Coml Committee Congress. This day taken up intirely in reading Letters of the cruelties committed by the Enemy in different places &c. And according to Costom very little Business done. P M. Marine Committee.

Wednesday, July 21

Coml Committee Congress. The Report on Duartee [Duarti] the Portugeze took up the whole day in debate.

> This was the culmination of a long and serious issue. Captain Joseph Cunningham of the private vessel *Phoenix* had captured a vessel owned by Duarti. Congress ordered restitution to Duarti and that those responsible be captured and brought to justice. Fell voted for the motion.

Thursday, July 22

Coml Committee Congress. After the dispatches were read, the order of the day on foreign affairs. long debates and some resolutions agreed to. Marine Committee Mr Camp

> Congress was still considering the proper way to proceed toward a peace treaty and the continuing issue of the fishery.

Friday, July 23

Coml Committee Congress. Letter from the Prisoners at Long Island, Referrd to a Committee of 3. Sundry Reports from the Board the Bd of War and Treasury, New Regulations in the Hide department &c. P M went to the Marine Committee Secretary not there

> These regulations provided for the appointment of a Commissary of Hides in individual states and the establishment of the salaries of the commissaries and their assistants and clerks.

Saturday, July 24

Commercial Committee Congress. Sundry Letters & Reports Genl Wilkinson was Balloted for Clothier General, Order of the day on foreighn affairs, after long debate as usual, and an amendmant offerd by Mr Dickinson the Previous Question was put by Mr McKean and carried

> This was a further attempt to resolve the fishery question, a matter with which Fell was about fed up. Neither Fell nor any other member of the New Jersey delegation is recorded as voting on the shutting off of debate.

Monday, July 26

Commercial Committee Congress. This day the particulars of the glorious affair of the taking the fort & Garrison at Stoney Point by Genl Wayne with his Letter & General Washingtons on the Occasion, with the Colours of the 17th Regt, were brought to Congress. Sundry dispatches were Read. (NB Mr Houston not at Congress)

> Congress was so pleased by this victory that resolutions of approval were passed for Washington, Wayne, and Wayne's officers, and special medals were ordered struck to commemorate the occasion.

Tuesday, July 27

Coml Committee Congress. After sundry Letters and dispatches were read the Report for the Officers to allow'd half Pay for Life and a further subsistance began to be debated Mr Houston my Colleague strongly oppos'd the motion.

> This matter is not mentioned in the *Journals* for this date.

Wednesday, July 28

Coml Committee. Congress. An acct from Minisink of a Number of Militia being cut off by the Indians & Col Hawthorn and some other Officers Killd. A very disagreeable and serious Memorial from the Minister of France complaining of Insults Offerd to the Consol General Mr Holker &c. Referrd to a Committee of 5. Order of the day on Finance some Regulations agreed to, for the Treasury Board

Thursday, July 29

Coml Committee Congress After the dispatches, Reports from the Board of War, and Treasury, the

The Journal

Order of the day was taken up on the Fishery, and according to Custom nothing done, no reasonable measures will satisfie the Eastern Members (Mr Mercier & Mr McCoomd [McComb] [).] P M Marine Committee.

> This was a continuation of the fishery question. Fell mentions that the eastern members could not be satisfied. It was, however, solid opposition from the South (Maryland, Virginia, North Carolina, and South Carolina) that is recorded in the *Journals.* Since the resolution approved provided for joint state action against Great Britain should she molest American fishermen after the war, the Southern states may have felt that they were committed to action over an issue which did not affect them. Mercier and McComb were elected Commissioners of Claims.

Friday, July 30

Coml Committee Congress. Finishd the Reports of the Board of Treasury Relative to Finance; The Report for allowing half Pay to the Officers for Life taken in to consideration. P M. Marine Committee

> An unsuccessful attempt was made by Houston of New Jersey and others to postpone consideration of the matter. Fell voted against his colleague on postponement.

Delegate from New Jersey

Saturday, July 31

Coml Committee   Congress   After reading some foreign Letters, Order of the day relating to the fishery, I hope for the last time

> Fell's impatience with this matter is obvious.

Sunday, August 1

Rainy day

Monday, August 2

Coml Committee   Congress   A long Letter from Mr Bingham and other dispatches took up this day. Mr Jay Sick

Tuesday, August 3

Coml Committee   Congress   Sundry Letters and Memorials Read, and some Resoluitions agreed to for Instructions.   P M Marine Committee

> The instructions mentioned here were for the American commissioners to the peace conference with Great Britain.

Wednesday, August 4

Coml Committee   Congress. A number of Letters from Genl Washington   Genl Gates &c. long debate on the Ministers memorial relating the Ship Mary & Elizabeth and the Report of the Committee thereon.

The Journal

This issue concerned the shipping of provisions out of states without permission. Congress concluded that the agent of the French King, Mr. Holker, was not guilty of any misconduct in the matter.

Thursday, August 5

Coml Committee   Congress. Some dispatches were read and the order of the day on the Ministers Memorial relating to Mr Holker   P M Marine Committee

> Congress agreed to notify the officials of Pennsylvania of the action taken on August 4 relative to Mr. Holker, but an attempt to have the resolution printed in the newspapers was defeated.

Friday, August 6

Coml Committee   Congress   Memorial from the Commisioners of the Treasury. Report to allow the Commisioners abroad 500 Sterlg by annum and their Expences. Motion for Silas Deane, Esqr. to be discharg'd from any further attendance on Congress and to setle his accounts & to be allowd for his Expences 3 Months after his Recall   Marine Committee

> In the *Journals* the allowances were quoted in *livres tournois* (11,428 per annum). The matter concerning Silas Deane was handled in two parts. The first, to allow him his expenses, was approved first. The

121

second, to excuse him from further attendance on Congress, was moved by Huntington and seconded by Fell. After two amendments, Fell, surprisingly, voted against the original motion.

Saturday, August 7

Coml Committee Congress. Motions amandments and long debate about instructions and an ultimatom.

> This was further discussion of a possible peace treaty with Great Britain.

Monday, August 9

Coml Committee Congress A New Plan for borrowing [blank] Millions on Loan 8 Ds for 5£s. debated & adjournd

> The *Journals* for this date do not mention any specifics of the proposed loan.

Tuesday, August 10

Coml Committee Congress Some dispatches motions, and debates. P M Marine Committee

> On this date Fell received $1,000 from the treasurer, the purpose of which was not stated.

Wednesday, August 11

Coml Committee Congress Report for better Proiding for the Army a motion was made by an

amendmant that the Resolve past May 24th, for half the Pay to the Officers for 7 Years should be extended for Life on the Question the Yaes & Naes being calld, it past in the affirmitive. P M Marine Committee

> The date should be May 15. Fell voted for the motion.

Thursday, August 12

Cl Committee Congress Report from the Committee on Coll Knobleck [Knobelauch] Memorial, Mr Scudder moved that he have 10,000 Ds. secconded by Mr McKean and 100 Guineas, Opposd the whole after debate Referrd to the Treasury. Mr Peabody secconded by Mr Schudder [Scudder] for all the Non Commissiond Officers and Soldiers to Recive half Pay for Life which opposd Referrd to a Committee of 5 P M Marine Committee.

> Lieutenant Colonel Knobelauch (Knaublauch) was recruited for American military service in Paris by Benjamin Franklin and Arthur Lee. Upon arriving in America, he found there was no proper position for him, and over a period of time he was reduced to severe poverty. He appealed to Congress to compensate him for his losses, particularly since he had rejected a British offer to serve in America in favor of American overtures. He estimated his expenses to have amounted to $12,000. The com-

Delegate from New Jersey

mittee report is printed in the *Journals* for August 7. Although there is no recorded vote, Fell apparently opposed paying him anything. Fell also opposed the measure for half pay for life for noncommissioned officers.

Friday, August 13

Coml Committee. Congress The day spent in Reading the Instructions for the Minister to be employd to Negotiate a Peace   P M. Marine Committee

> These instructions are printed in the *Journals* for August 14.

Saturday, August 14

Coml Committee   Congress Draft of a Letter to the States, agreed. to fill their Batallions and hold their Militia in readiness. Motion made by Mr Gerry to Adress Ireland to Revolt on the Question house divided it was Lost

> This letter revealed that the British were sending some 10,000 additional troops to America. It appealed to the states to fill their military quotas and to be ready for attack. In addition, the letter stated that America's allies were disturbed to learn that early adequate preparations had not been made. No explanation is given in the *Journals* on the Irish matter. Apparently, there was hope for an Irish rebellion that

124

would take British pressure off the United States.

Monday, August 16

Coml Committee   Congress. Letters, Memorials &c. A very extraordinary motion was made to postpone the Resolution for half pay for Life to the Officers to make way for a Motion for the States to provide for them in their own way

> This matter is not discussed in detail in the *Journals*. It seems that Fell considered it very unusual for the states to be responsible for soldiers' pensions.

Tuesday, August 17

P M   Sett off for Petersfield and Returnd to Philadelphia in the morning of Monday August the 30th. Congress. the day chiefly spent in debates about, and reading A Lees & Wm Lees Letters from France

> Although there are no specific details, Fell apparently went home for a vacation of almost two weeks.

Tuesday, August 31

Commercial Committee   Congress. This day spent in a disagreeable complaint of Mr Lawrence [Laurens] against Secretary Thompson [Thomson] others Join'd, at last a Committee was appointed to hear the parties P M. Marine Committee

Laurens stated that he believed that he had been treated with disrespect by the Secretary of Congress. The committee was ordered to hear both sides.

Wednesday, Sept. 1

Coml Committee. Congress. After some time spent in reading A Lees Letters it was propos'd and carried for postponing to take up the order on finance, in regard to stoping the press. after debate the previous Question was call'd for by Mr Lawrence [Laurens] and the Yaes & Naes call'd carried againt it the Motion was that on no acct more than 200000000 should be Ėmited, and that 40 Million of that sum should not be emited provided the States would supply it, the Question was divided and agreed to stop the Press. near 5 oClock.

> The reading of Lee's letter was postponed to take up a report from the Finance Committee. This was then postponed to consider the matter of currency. The discussion here revolved around the amount of money to be printed. Congress decided that $200 million would be the maximum. The $40 million which would raise the amount to the $200 million total would not be printed if it "can be obtained by other means." Fell says that it should come from the states.

The Journal

Thursday, Sept. 2

C Committee   Congress. This day chiefly lost in reading the ridicolous Letters of Mr A Lee. P M Marine Committee

> Fell was obviously disgusted with the whole Deane-Lee controversy. The *Journals* show that Fell seconded a motion to postpone the reading, but it failed.

Friday, Sept. 3

Coml Committee   Congress. This day the Question was finaly decided almost unanimouly not to Emit any more Bills then will amount to 200 Million of Dollars. And a Committee of 5 were appointed to frame a Circular Letter to the Legislatures of the different States, for the purpose of raising the Supplys by Taxes and Loans. P M Marine Committee

> On September 8, the President of Congress was asked to write the circular letter. The letter is printed in the *Journals* for September 13.

Saturday, Sept. 4

Commercial Committee   Congress. Did not attend Congress this day having been employ'd at the Commercial Committee in examing the Books &c. Last night W. H. Drayton Died.

> Drayton died of a cause requiring burial within twenty-four hours. Congress attended his funeral as a body.

Monday, Sept. 6

Coml Committee   Congress   Sundry Letters Memorials & Petitions   P M Marine Committee

Tuesday, Sept. 7

Coml Committee   Congress. A number of Letters, One from the Duke DeVirgenes [Comte de Vergennes] advising of his suspicions, of making Peace without his Court. Refferd to a Committee of three vizt. [blank]

> The letter was sent to Congress by Gerard. The committee consisted of Houston, Mathews, and Huntington.

Wednesday, Sept. 8

Coml Committee   Congress. This day spent in Reading dispatches, &c. A Memorial from the State of New York, relating to the disputes with Vermont   Refferd to a Committee of 5 vizt. McKean, Paca, Houlton [Holten], Huntington & Smith

> The Vermont question still concerned possible statehood.

Thursday, Sept. 9

Commercial Committee   Congress. This day I nominated Wm Denning, Esqr. to be appointed a Commissioner for the Board of Treasury. P M Marine Committee.

The Journal

Fell seldom spoke in Congress or made motions. Denning's name appears on October 12 in the *Journals* as one of the nominees, but it was erased. The reason is not given.

Friday, Sept. 10

Commercial Committee Congress. Sundry Letters &c. Report from the Board of War for the States to provide Cloathing for their Troops &c. Reports from Mr Dickinson for a Negotiation with Spain, another by Mr Huntington. P M Marine Committee

> Dickinson's motion is recorded in the *Journals* on September 9. It concerned the attempts to bring Spain into the war. Huntington's motion on September 10 guaranteed the Floridas to Spain in return for free navigation of the Mississippi River if she would enter the war.

Saturday, Sept. 11

Coml Committee Congress. This whole day taken up in the proposals for a nigotiation with spain.

> Congress approved Huntington's resolution of the previous day.

Monday, Sept. 13

Coml Committee Congress. A great number of dispatches took up the whole day till 5 oClock.

Delegate from New Jersey

Dined with Governor Levingston [Livingston] at Mr Jays.

Tuesday, Sept. 14

Commercial Committee Congress. Two memorials were read relating to the Lands of Indiana and [blank] Signd by [blank] Trent & Geo Morgon [Morgan], Mr Scudder moved for the first Memorial being Committed, after long debate on the part of Virginia to oppose it, the Question was put and Pas'd in the affirmitive then the Delegates from Virginia made a Motion that Congress had no right to interfere in the afair at all, and had no jurisdiction nor right to appoint a Committee the Delegates of No Carolina and from So Carolina made objections to Vote and were joind by the President under a notion that the Lands in Question were intended to be seperate States long debates till Adjournd Did not attend the Marine Committee being unwell

> The first blank space in the diary should read Vandalia. Trent's first name was William. Morgan's letter concerned the Indiana tract and Trent's Vandalia. The long debate was on the right of Virginia to claim this territory under its original grant from the King of England. This was a part of the larger question of western land claims which vexed Congress for so long. The question of ownership of this territory delayed the ratification of the Articles of

The Journal

Confederation. Morgan's letter requested that Congress rule that western land was national territory. Fell seconded Scudder's motion. The *Journals* do not record the motion of Virginia nor the long debates Fell mentioned.

Wednesday, Sept. 15

Commercial Committee Congress After reading the Journals, the Delegates moved for their motion made Yesterday to be Enterd which caused a long debate on point of order and I not being well I left Congress.

> This was probably the Virginia motion of the day before. The *Journals* are totally silent on this matter.

Saturday, Sept. 25

First day I went abroad since being Sick. It was moved that Minister to Negotiate a Peace with great Britain and a great deal of disagreeable altercation and debate occasioned by Mr Lees being so often mention'd at last Mr Jay Mr Adams and Mr Lee were put in Nomination, Adjournd

> Fell did not attend the sessions of Congress from September 15 to September 25 because of illness. Arthur Lee, constantly mentioned as a possible nominee, continued to cause great concern because of his struggle with Deane and his meddling in our relations with France, much to the

131

annoyance of Benjamin Franklin. Fell says that Lee was nominated on September 25 for the position, but the *Journals* record that Henry Laurens nominated him the next day.

Sunday, Sept. 26

Congress met. great debates as before, Balloted. Mr Adams 5. Mr Jay 4. Mr Lee 1. no Choice. Balloted 2d time Mr Adams 6 Mr Jay 5. no Election.

> The *Journals* record that three votes were taken, but they do not record the tally. The Confederation required that seven states were necessary for election. When the election was postponed, another proposal was made and passed that a minister plenipotentiary to Spain be appointed to negotiate an alliance and a commercial treaty. This was a virtual repudiation of Arthur Lee, the current minister.

Monday, Sept. 27

Coml Committee Congress. Agreed that a Minister Plenoptentiary be appointed for the Court of Spain Mr Jay was appointed Agreed that a Minister Plenoptentiary be appointed to negotiate a Peace with great Britain Mr Adams was Elected.

> The decision to appoint a minister to Spain reaffirmed the action taken the previous

The Journal

day. The *Journals* record no debate on the question or on the appointment of Jay and Adams.

Tuesday, Sept. 28

C. Committee The Congress. Elected a New President by Ballot vizt. Mr Huntington. A Secretary for the Embasey were put in nomination vizt. Mr Carmichael by Mr Searle. P M Marine Committee Dined wth Jos. Wharton

> John Jay, having been elected Minister to Spain, resigned his office as President of Congress. Congress decided to appoint a secretary for each of the Ministers to Spain, Britain, and France. Carmichael and Searle were nominated for Spain. However, Searle's name was erased from the *Journals* with the notation: "withdrawn." Three nominations were also made for Great Britain and two for France.

Wednesday, Sept. 29

C. C. Congress. After the dispatches, Reports from the Board of War and Treasury were finishd then Balloted for a Secretary For Mr Jay, when the Votes for Mr Carmichael were unanimous, Candidates for Mr. Adams Secretary were Mr John Trumbull Mr Jonathan Trumbull [Jr.] and Mr Dana, first Ballot John Trumbull had 4 Votes Mr Dana 6. second Ballot Mr Dana 7—he was Elected. For Secretary to Dr Franklin the Candi-

133

dates Mr Thull and Mr Laurens, Mr Laurens had Eleven Votes and was Elected. A Commissioner to Examine the accts. in France was appointed, the Candidates were Mr Edmd Jennings Mr Laboushire [Labouchere] & Mr Joshua Johnson first Ballot 1 . . . 3 6
second do [ballot] 4 7
Mr Johnson was Ellected. A Report was brought in from the Committee, to allow the Minister Plenoptentiary £3000 Sterlg by annum and the Secretary £1000 Sterlg by Do [annum] Postponed

> Franklin's secretary was John Laurens, son of Henry Laurens. The election of secretaries is recorded in the *Journals,* but there is no mention of the actual vote or number of ballots. Congress had authorized a commissioner to settle the dispute over Silas Deane's accounts in France on August 6; the nominations were made on September 28. Johnson was supposedly a close friend of Deane's; thus, he might be expected to report favorably to Deane.

Thursday, Sept. 30

Commercial Committee   Congress. A number of Letters Memorials &c. were read. P M Marine Committee   Capt Read appointed to the Frigate Bourbon.

Friday, Oct. 1

Coml Committee. Congress. Several Letters &c. Read. Genl Arnolds accts. of his Expences for

9 Mo. Extravigant indeed Committed to 5 vizt. [blank] Moved for the thanks of the House to be given our late President Mr Jay. agreed.

> The committee on Arnold's accounts was composed of Laurens, Mercer, Peabody, Holten, and Paca. The motion to honor John Jay was made by Fell.

Saturday, Oct. 2

Com. Committee Congress. After reading the Journals went into the order of the day which was for the house to goe in to a Committee of the whole house on Finance.

Monday, Oct. 4

Commercial Committee Congress. This day spent in Reading dispatches Memorials, Treasury Reprts &c. NB a great tumult in the City and some Lives Lost several Wounded and several sent to Goal

> This was known as the "Fort Wilson Riot" in Philadelphia.

Tuesday, Oct. 5

Coml Committee Congress. A very long Letter from Genl Sulevan [Sullivan] was Read giving an account of his Expidition in to the Indian Country, distroying 40 Towns &c. &c. On the Report from the Committee to ascertain the Sallery by

Delegate from New Jersey

Annum of the Minister Plenoptentiary and the Secretary

Motion first   for £3000 Sterl.   Ayes 3 Noes 3. Divided 4

do [motion]   for £2500 do [Sterl.] do [Ayes] 5. do [Noes] 3. do [Divided] 2

do [motion] for Secretary 1000 do [Sterl.] do [Ayes] 5. do [Noes] 3. do [Divided] 3

P M Marine Committee

> The decision on salaries is recorded in the *Journals* under October 4. The authority on the Continental Congress, Edmund C. Burnett, believes that Fell may be correct and the *Journals* in error. See his *Letters of Members of the Continental Congress*, IV, 474n.

Wednesday, Oct. 6

Coml Committee Congress. After the dispatches were Read a Committee of 12 was appointed for the apportening the Quotas for the payment of the 15 Million.

Thursday, Oct. 7

Coml Committee Congress. The Committee of 12 brought in a Report as follows viz.

NB the Delegates from New Jersey as well as some other States did all they could to lower their sums but all in vain.

                    Ds.

New Hampshire	400,000
Massachusets	2300,000
Rhode Island	200,000
Connecticut	1700,000
New York	750,000
New Jersey	900,000
Philadelphia	2300,000
Delaware	170,000
Maryland	1580,000
Virginia	2500,000
No Carolina	1000,000
So Carolonia	1200,000
	15,000,000

P M Marine Committee

> Fell's entry for Philadelphia should be Pennsylvania.

Friday, Oct. 8

Coml Committee. Congress. Letter from General Washington, relating to [blank] The Memorials of G Morgan and Trent, Respecting the Lands of Indiana and [blank] Refferd to a Committee of 5. Several Reports from the Treasury &c. Marine Committee

> Washington's letter referred to the matter of cooperation with the Comte d'Estaing.

The letters of Morgan and Trent related to Indiana and Vandalia.

Saturday, Oct. 9

Coml Committee Congress. After the dispatches were Read the Committee on Ways and meas brought in a draft of a Letter to be sent to the Governours and President of Each State for the Requisition of the 15 Million &c. the Committee brought in the draught of Commission and Letter of Credence for the Secretary appointed to go to Spain

Sunday, Oct. 10

Dined at Frankford.

Monday, Oct. 11

Commercial Committee. Sundry Letters Memorials &c. A Memorial from the Legislature of New Jersey relating to fixing the price of Produce &c. Committed to a Member from Each State.

Tuesday, Oct. 12

Commercial Committee Congress. Letter from Coll Broadhead [Brodhead] giving an acct. of his Transactions and Expedition againt the Indians &c. Moved that the Commissioners &c. for the Board of Treasury hold their Offices during Pleasure. P M Marine Committee

The Journal

The decision about terms of office for the Treasury Board is not mentioned in the *Journals* for October 12, but it is discussed on October 23.

Wednesday, Oct. 13

Coml Committee   Congress. Dispatches, Letters & Memorials were Read, Also Reports from the Board of Treasury. Dr Weatherspoon [Witherspoon] moved for the Ultimatom in the Instructions to the Minister of Spain, instead of insisting on the Free Navigation of the Missisipi to have a free Port only   6 ayes 4 Noes 1 devided.

> Fell apparently reversed the vote since the *Journals* record the vote as 4 yes, 6 no, and 1 divided.

Thursday, Oct. 14

Coml Committee   Congress. Long debates about the title to be given the President of Congress whether Excellency or Honor and the filling up the Secretary Commission. Dr Wetherspoon [Witherspoon] not in Congress, State not Represented   P M. Marine Committee

> The discussion about titles is not mentioned in the *Journals*.

Friday, Oct. 15

Coml Committee   Congress. Mr Jay requested leave for Lt Coll Levingston [Henry Brockholst

139

Livingston] to goe with him to Spain, a furloe was granted for 12 Months   Marine Committee

Saturday, Oct. 16

Coml Committee. Congress. After the dispatches &c. were read, Congress went in to a Committee of the whole on a Report for obtaining a Loan for 5 Million of Dollars and having the same sold in Bills of Exchange or laid out in the purchase of Goods to be disposed of by order of Congress, with a long train of Commissionors &c. after debate adjourn'd

> No final decision was made on this matter.

Monday, Oct. 18

Coml Committee   Congress. after the dispatches, went in to a Committee of the whole when the Loan was agreed to & some persons put in nomination, for Negotiating the Loan and a long debate about Importing the Goods.

> The *Journals* report that no final decision was made about the loan. Three names were put into nomination to negotiate a loan in Holland, and a committee was appointed to prepare instructions for the person who might be appointed.

Tuesday, Oct. 19

Coml Committee   Congress. After the dispatches, went in to a Committee of the whole, when the

The Journal

Question was put abt Importing the Goods carried in the Negative by a great Majority Afterwards a printed Report of an other Committee was read, (full of complexd Idieas) Committe Rose and had leave to sitt again. After some motions made in Congress Adjournd; Mr Huston [Houston] came today P M Marine Committee

Wednesday, Oct. 20

Coml Committee Congress. A number of dispatches Reports from Committees &c. A Report for the form of the prayer to be used on Thursday the day of Decr. was read and agreed too, (Mr Huston [Houston] gone home having had an acct of the death of his Child)

> The second Thursday in December was designated as a day of Thanksgiving.

Thursday, Oct. 21

Coml Committee Congress. Some dispatches and several Reports from Committees, Order of the day for Balloting for a person to be sent to Europe to Negotate a Loan Mr Laurens was appointed Mr Laurens 8 Votes, Mr Adams 3. (NB. Mr Scudder [)]

> No actual vote is recorded in the *Journals*.
> Scudder returned to Congress.

Friday, Oct. 22

Coml Committee   Congress, Memorials, Letter Treasury Reports &c.

Saturday, Oct. 23

Com Committee   Congress. After the dispatches the order of the day on the Report for the Sallerys of the Treasury Bd. agreed as follows   That the Commissioners and other Officers have their places during Pleasure. (Resolve past some time since that the Election should be annual)
Sallerys by annum

Treasurer	15000 Dolls.
Commissioners of the Board of Treasurey	14000
Auditor General	12000
Commissioners of Chamber of Accounts	12000
Assistant Auditor General	10000
Secretary to the Board of Treasurey	10000
Clerks in the above Offices	7000

> This decision provided that they would serve at the pleasure of Congress regardless of other provisions that may have been made.

Sunday, Oct. 24

Rainy Day.

Monday, Oct. 25

Coml Committee   Congress. Letter from Genl Washington dated 21st advising that the Enemy had Evacuated Stoney and Verplancks Point, and Reported they were going to leave Rhode Island, Report from the Committee with Instructions to Mr Laurens to Negotiate a Loan

Tuesday, Oct. 26

Coml Committee. Congress After some dispatches were Read the Report for Instructions to Mr Laurens was taken up and debated the whole day to no purpose   P M   Marine Committee   NB Dr Weatherspoon [Witherspoon]   Confederacy and Eagle Packet Saild this day from the Capes

> Witherspoon returned to Congress after being absent since October 14.

Wednesday, Oct. 27

Coml Committee   Congress. Several Memorials Letters & Reports from Board of War and Treasurey. A Report from the Medical Committee for further Provision for the Director General   Surgeon   Phisicians &c. in the Army for Subsistance Cloathing &c.

Thursday, Oct. 28

Coml Committee   Congress. After the dispatches, A Report from the Marine Committee was taken

Delegate from New Jersey

up to Establish a Board of Admiralty consisting of 3 not Members of Congress as Commissioners & two Members of Congress with a Secretary. Sallery of the Commissioners 14000 Ds by annum and Secretary 10,000.

Friday, Oct. 29

Coml Committee Congress. After the dispatches &c. were Read, the Committee to whom was Referrd the Memorials of Coll Morgon [Morgan] and Coll Treat [Trent] Respecting Lands claimd by Virginia brought in a Report, which Virginia objected to on which a long debate ensuid. P M Marine Committee

> The committee recommended that Virginia and other states with western land claims should suspend all sales, grants, and settlements in the disputed areas until the war was over.

Saturday, Oct. 30

Coml Committee Congress. Resolved to Reccomend to the State of Virginia not to dispose of any unlocated Lands &c.

Monday, Nov. 1

Coml Committee Congress. The Instructions & Commission for Mr Laurens, his Sallery £1500 Sterlg and a Secretary £300. Sterlg Dr Wetherspoon [Witherspoon] gone home

Tuesday, Nov. 2

Coml Committee   This day a doubt ariseing whether the Connecticut Delegates could set after the first Monday in this month, and not being Members sufficient without them no Business was done.

Wednesday, Nov. 3

Coml Committee   This day no Business done for the reasons mentiond Yesterday

Thursday, Nov. 4

Coml Committee   The Secretary did Business today in the absence of the President. P M Marine Committee

Friday, Nov. 5

Coml Committee   Congress. Letter from Genl Gates acquainting that he took Possesion of Rhode Island the 26th Octr the Enemy having left it the day before   P M Marine Committee

Saturday, Nov. 6

Commercial Committee   Congress. After the dispatches &c. a Report of the Committee to answer the Speech intended to be made by the Chevalier Lasern [Chevalier de la Luzerne] was Read.

> The Chevalier de la Luzerne, the new minister from France, had sent ahead of

Delegate from New Jersey

him his credentials and a copy of his first public speech. Congress considered the speech and a proper answer to it.

Monday, Nov. 8

Coml Committee   Congress. The Report of the answer to the Ministers Speech was agreed to.

Tuesday, Nov. 9

Coml Committee   Congress Agreeable to the order of the Day Balloted for Commissioners of Treasury Board vizt. Appointed [blank] Forman [Foreman] [blank] Turnbull [Jonathan Trumbull, Jr.], John Gibson [erased] Auditor of Accts. Millegen [James Milligan]=Deputy Auditor General

> Fell does not include all the elections this day, and his account is partly inaccurate. Elected Commissioners of the Treasury Board were Ezekiel Foreman and Jonathan Trumbull, Jr. There was no office of Auditor of Accounts. John Gibson, the name Fell erased, was Auditor-General under the old system. James Milligan was chosen Auditor-General. Other elections also occurred this day.

Wednesday, Nov. 10

Coml Committee   Congress. President Huntington in the Chair   This day Receivd from Genl Lincoln the disagreeable acct of Count De Estaing

Raising the Seige of Savanna in Georgia. Mr Hewes Died this day

> Congress resolved to attend as a body the funeral of Hewes.

Thursday, Nov. 11

Coml Committee   This day chiefly spent in debate about the sending some Troops and Stores to So Carolina   P M attended the funeral of Mr Hewes

Friday, Nov. 12

Coml Committee   Congress. Reports from the Board of War and Treasury:
Balloted for a Commissioner of Treasury Board

	1st	2d	3d	4
Wm Denning	5 Votes	6.	5.	4
John Gibson	6		5.	5. 6
John Milligen [James Milligan]	1	. .	1	. . . .

Marine Committee.

> There is no record of this vote in the *Journals*. The record shows that on November 25 John Gibson was elected, but no other candidates are mentioned. Fell records this in his diary on November 24.

Saturday, Nov. 13

Com Committee. Congress. A Letter from Genl Sulevan [Sullivan] to Resign Referrd to a Committee, Letter from Coll Webb for leave for Genl

Delegate from New Jersey

Philips [Phillips] & Genl Redsell [Riedesel] to go to New York   Majr Genl Green [Greene] Quarter Mastr General Rece'd from April 6th. 1778 to Octr 20th 1779   62583,571. 30/90

> Sullivan wished to resign for health reasons. The meaning of the figures included here is not clear.

Monday, Nov. 15

Coml Committee. Sundry Letters &c. Motion from Mr Gerry that no member of Congress, should hold any office or be chose while a Member or for 6 Mo after   Nominated Gentlemen for the Admiralty Board

Tuesday, Nov. 16

Com. Committee. Letter from Commisary Baety [Beatty] relating to Citizens Prisoners &c. Referrd to a Committee   Dr Wetherspoon [Witherspoon]

> Witherspoon returned to Congress, having been absent since November 1.

Wednesday, Nov. 17

Com Committee   This day at 12 oClock The Chevalier DeLaLuserne [de la Luzerne] the Minister Plenoptentiary from France had his Audience of Congress,

> His speech is printed in French and English in the *Journals*.

The Journal

Thursday, Nov. 18

Com Com   Congress. Sundry Letters Memorials and Reports, One from the Committee of 12 in Order to Regulate prices was Read & debated

> This concerned the request of New Jersey for price regulation.

Friday, Nov. 19

Com. Com. Congress. Report for regulating prices @ 20 for 1   agreed to for all home Manufactories &c. and all imported articles to bear a proportion to the above   Marine Committee

> Congress recommended to the states that prices be set at no more than twenty times the rate in 1774.

Saturday, Nov. 20

Coml Committee   Congress. The Resolution brought in to Reccomend to the States the altering the Law for obliging Creds to take the money for Debts, long debated and Postponed   Report of the Medical Committee   Rain

> This debate is not mentioned in the *Journal* for November 20. It was postponed on the previous day.

Monday, Nov. 22

Com. Com   Congress. After the dispatches, Committee on ways and means brought in a Report, to

149

Delegate from New Jersey

draw Bills on Mr Laurens and Mr Jay for £100000 Sterlg Each after long debate[.] agreed to go in a Committee of the whole house to morrow: Mr Griffin and Mr Harnet were appointed to the Commercial Committee.

Tuesday, Nov. 23

Com. Committee Congress. This day Resolved to draw Bills on Mr Jay and Mr Lawrence [Laurens] for £200000 Sterlg @ 6 Mo. sight. I was against the measure

> Fell was the only member of the New Jersey delegation to vote against the measure.

Wednesday, Nov. 24

Com. Com Congress Sundry Letters Reports &c. Mr Gibson was Elected to the Treasury Bd.

Gibson	Millen [Milligan]	Denning
5	6	
6	5	
6	2	2
8		2

> This election without mention of other candidates or ballots is recorded in the *Journals* on November 25.

Thursday, Nov. 25

Com. Com. Congress. Several dispatches, Reports of Committees, Board of War Treasury (Snow)

150

Friday, Nov. 26

Commercial Committee. Congress. Letter from General Washington with the State of the army &c. Sundry Letters &c. Elected two Members for the Admiralty Board viz. Mr Warring [Waring] and Mr. Whiple [Whipple]

Saturday, Nov. 27

Com Com Congress. Several Reports Read and debated NB Dined with Mr Griffin

Monday, Nov. 29

Com. Com Committee Reported respecting the Bills to be drawn and after several amendments the Yeas and Noes were calld carried in the affirmitive. I was No.

Tuesday, Nov. 30

Com. Com Congress. Some dispatches were Read, after moved for finishing the appointment of another Commissioner for the Admiralty Board which caused a long debate and nothing done General Sulevans [Sullivan] Resignation was accepted. Commercial Committee gave in a Report to Put that in Commission by the Style of the Board of Trade.

BRIEF BIOGRAPHIES

Adams, John. Second President of the United States, he had a long and illustrious career. After serving in the Continental Congress during the turbulent first years of Revolution, he was elected commissioner to France in 1778. Later in the year he was replaced when Benjamin Franklin was named sole plenipotentiary as a result of the Deane-Lee controversy. In September 1779 Adams was appointed minister to negotiate peace and commercial treaties with Great Britain.

Adams, Samuel. He was one of the most important and influential revolutionary agitators in the period leading to the break with Great Britain. His effective career lasted only from the beginning of the quarrel to the Declaration of Independence. He served in Congress until 1781 and was instrumental in drafting the Articles of Confederation. However, his record and service after Independence were somewhat undistinguished.

Adams, Thomas. He was a member of Congress from Virginia from 1778 to 1780. A businessman in England

Brief Biographies

before the Revolution, he returned in 1774 to Virginia, where he became an active member of the Revolutionary movement. He remained active in state affairs until his death.

Aitken, Robert. A Philadelphia printer, he was imprisoned in 1777 for his support of the Revolution. He published the *Pennsylvania Magazine, or American Monthly Museum* in 1775-1776 and printed the first American Bible in 1782.

Allen, Ethan. He was a revolutionary soldier whose life is most often associated with the attempts of Vermont to obtain recognition as a separate state. At the outbreak of war in 1775, he and Benedict Arnold led the successful attack on Fort Ticonderoga. Later in the year he was captured by the British during the expedition against Canada. After his exchange in 1778, he unsuccessfully presented the Vermont claims to the Continental Congress. In 1780 he was associated with an attempt to make Vermont a province of Great Britain. The question of his loyalty in this matter has never been settled.

Allison, John. A member of the Virginia state militia, he was promoted to lieutenant colonel in 1779 at his own request.

Armand, Charles Treflin, Marquis de la Rouaire. A French soldier, he volunteered for service in the American Revolution in 1777. He was an effective officer and a severe critic of General Gates for his defeat at Camden.

Delegate from New Jersey

Armstrong, John. A surveyor from Pennsylvania, he entered the military during the Revolution with a very prestigious reputation dating from the French and Indian War. His service in the Revolution never lived up to his reputation. He served in the Continental Congress in 1779-1780 and 1787-1788.

Arnold, Benedict. He is best known as the traitor who betrayed military secrets to the British. Following the Battle of Saratoga, he was placed in command of Philadelphia in June 1778 after the British had evacuated the city. He immediately ran into difficulties. His social obligations drove him into debt, and he was in trouble with local officials. He was also charged with using military equipment and men for personal use. After demanding a court-martial, he was judged guilty of misusing military supplies and of employing military personnel for menial personal duties. It was at this time in 1779 that he began his relationship with the British that eventually led to his treason.

Ashmead, John. He was the captain of the Pennsylvania privateer *Eagle*. Sent to the West Indies to acquire powder by the Marine Committee, he was able to obtain it, but it was far below the quality anticipated.

Atlee, Samuel John. Born in New Jersey, he was a delegate to Congress from Pennsylvania from 1778 to 1782. During the French and Indian War he acquired military experience which he put to good use in the Revolution. He was captured by the British at the Battle of Long Island in 1776 and was held prisoner until 1778, when he was exchanged. Following his Congressional service, he remained active in Pennsylvania affairs, particularly in dealing with the Indians.

Brief Biographies

Baylor, George. A Virginian by birth, he began his Revolutionary service as an aide to General Washington. He was later promoted to the rank of colonel and given command of a regiment of cavalry. In 1778 he suffered a serious defeat and was taken prisoner. Although there is some question about Baylor's conduct in this engagement, no action was taken against him.

Beatty, John. He was a Revolutionary soldier from New Jersey. After studying medicine with Benjamin Rush, he joined the Revolutionary forces in 1776. Captured at the Battle of Fort Washington in 1776, he was badly mistreated until his exchange in 1778. Because of this experience he was appointed Commissary General of Prisoners in 1779. He was arrested and tried in 1780 for trading with the enemy; he resigned his commission as a result. He was later a delegate to the Continental Congress in 1784-1785.

Beaumarchais, Pierre Augustin Caron de. A French author, he became active in commercial ventures, which made him a fortune. He advocated aid for the American colonies as early as 1775. He made arrangements with the American commissioner Silas Deane to sell supplies to the Americans in 1777. This was done under the cover of a private company, but in truth it was secret aid from the French Crown. After the French alliance was made Arthur Lee, another commissioner, argued that the supplies had been gifts. This was the beginning of the Deane-Lee dispute, which continued for several years.

Bedlow, William. He was Auditor of Accounts for the Eastern Department of the Continental Army. In

August 1779 he brought charges of misconduct against James Geary, Deputy Clothier-General of the Northern Department.

Bingham, William. He was the British consul at St. Pierre, Martinique, from 1770 to 1776. After the Revolution began he remained for four years as American agent in the West Indies. His reports proved very valuable to the Continental Congress. He later served in the Continental Congress from Pennsylvania in 1786-1789 and in the United States Senate in 1795-1801. His greatest contribution was in banking and in increasing the stability of American finance.

Bland, Theodorick. He was a doctor and planter from Virginia who became a military officer during the Revolution. In 1778 he was ordered to command the transfer and guarding of the prisoners taken in the Battle of Saratoga. He remained in this post until 1779. He later served in the Continental Congress and the First Congress under the Constitution.

Brackenridge, Hugh Henry. He was a minister in Philadelphia who delivered the oration on July 5, 1779, in the German Calvinist Church. Entitled "An Eulogium of the brave men who have fallen in the contest with Great Britain," it received a letter of praise from General Washington.

Bradford, William, Jr. A jurist from Pennsylvania, he answered the call of duty by serving in the military during the Revolution. He served as Deputy Muster Master General in the Continental Army from 1777 to 1779. He saw much active service, but his health was so

Brief Biographies

impaired that he was forced to resign in 1779. He later served in state and national judicial positions.

Bretigny, Marquis de. He was one of the many French volunteers in the Revolution. On January 1, 1779, he communicated to George Washington a plan for raising a French regiment to fight in the war.

Brodhead, Daniel. At the outbreak of the Revolution, he served in the Pennsylvania militia. In 1778 he was sent as a part of General Lachlan McIntosh's command at Fort Pitt. After his opposition had helped to remove McIntosh, he replaced him as commander. He carried out successful raids against the Delaware Indians to the north.

Brower, ———. He, along with Loziers, had been arrested by Sir Henry Clinton for killing a Loyalist named Richards. Washington protested that they were being treated too severely and requested that they be treated as any other prisoners-of-war.

Burke, Thomas. Representing North Carolina in the Continental Congress from 1776 to 1781, he was one of the most active and important members. He was particularly critical of Congressional secrecy and very suspicious of military power which seemed to threaten civil rights. A severe critic of the Articles of Confederation, he was responsible for Article II of the document which reserved to the states powers not delegated to the national government. In 1781 he was elected Governor of North Carolina.

Cadwalader, Lambert. Born in New Jersey, he was a prominent businessman in Philadelphia before the Revolution. He served in various civil offices in the early stages of the Independence movement and later as a military officer, until his resignation in 1779. Afterwards he sat in the Continental Congress and the new Congress under the Constitution.

Camp, Caleb. A resident of Morristown, New Jersey, he was a member of the New Jersey Legislature from Essex County.

Campbell, Sir Archibald. A British soldier, he was imprisoned for a time in retaliation for mistreatment of American soldiers by the British. In 1778 he led the expedition against Savannah which resulted in the capture of the city. In 1779 he also took Augusta but, unable to hold it, he retreated to Savannah.

Carmichael, William. He was a member of the Continental Congress from Maryland from 1778 to 1780. Prior to his election, he had served as a diplomat in Europe, including service as an aide to Silas Deane. In 1779 he was chosen by Congress as secretary to John Jay, newly-elected minister to Spain. When Jay left Spain in 1782, Carmichael remained in charge of the American mission. His greatest contribution was in representing American interests in Spain until his death in 1795.

Celeron, Lewis. A Canadian-born officer, he served in the Continental Army with the rank of captain. In the field almost continually and unable to look after his personal affairs, he suffered financial reverses. He appealed to Congress for financial restitution and a promotion in rank. On February 20, 1779, he was awarded $1,000 but no promotion.

Brief Biographies

Clark, Abraham. A signer of the Declaration of Independence from New Jersey, he was a surveyor and lawyer. An early convert to the patriot cause, he served both in New Jersey offices and in the Continental Congress. He was an outspoken man with numerous enemies, but he rendered conspicuous service to the cause of Independence.

Clarke, Elijah. A soldier from South Carolina, he served in various areas in the South. On several occasions his good judgment prevented defeat at the hands of the enemy.

Clarkson, Matthew. An army officer from New York, he served in the Battle of Long Island and as aide-de-camp to Benedict Arnold in 1778-1779. In this position he was constantly in conflict with Pennsylvania and Philadelphia officials due to his and Arnold's actions in the defense of the area. After the war he became a prominent businessman and philanthropist.

Clinton, George. Vice President under Jefferson and Madison, Clinton had one of the most solidly useful careers of any man of his age. He was active in the pre-Revolutionary period, served in the Continental Congress, and was a brigadier general in the Continental Army. From 1777 to 1795 he was the first governor of the state of New York.

Clinton, Sir Henry. After acquiring military experience in New York and Europe, he was appointed second in command to Sir William Howe in attempting to put down the American Revolution. When Howe returned to England in 1778, Clinton became commander in chief of British forces in North America. He evacuated Philadelphia and concentrated his actions in New York. In 1781 he resigned his command and returned to Britain.

Collins, John. He was a member of the Continental Congress from Rhode Island from 1778 to 1783. As Governor of Rhode Island from 1786 to 1790, he cast the deciding vote to call a convention to consider ratification of the Constitution.

Condict, Silas. A leader in New Jersey affairs, he served on the state council from its organization in 1776 until 1780. He was probably one of the men who carried the message from New Jersey to the Continental Congress on May 21, 1779. He later served in the Continental Congress from 1781 to 1784.

Conyngham, Gustavus. An American naval captain, he was held in confinement by the British in New York. Upon petition from his wife, Congress directed a letter to the commander at New York demanding proper and humane treatment for him. Congress also threatened to hold in close confinement a number of British prisoners to assure his safe treatment.

Cox, John. He was Assistant Quartermaster-General of the Continental Army under Nathaniel Greene. A close friend, Greene insisted that Cox and Charles Pettit be appointed as his assistants before he would accept the position of Quartermaster-General.

Dana, Francis. He was a member of the Continental Congress from Massachusetts, 1776-1778 and 1784. From 1774 to 1776 he had been in England trying to adjust

Brief Biographies

differences between Great Britain and the colonies. In 1779 he was chosen as secretary of the delegation headed by John Adams to negotiate a peace treaty with Great Britain. He later served as Minister to Russia, but was never received by that government. Beginning in 1791 for fifteen years he was Chief Justice of the Massachusetts Supreme Court.

Deane, Silas. An early Revolutionary leader in Connecticut, he served in both the First and Second Continental Congresses. In 1776 he was appointed the first American foreign representative. Acting under authority of two Congressional committees, he acquired military supplies with the aid of Caron de Beaumarchais. He also commissioned many foreign soldiers for American service, some very able and many merely adventurers. In September 1776 Benjamin Franklin and Arthur Lee were sent to France to aid him. In 1778 Deane was recalled by Congress to answer charges made by Arthur Lee that the material acquired was meant as a gift from the French government. Lee charged that Deane and Beaumarchais were profiteering on the transaction. This dispute took much of the time of Congress for two years. Because of unavailable documents, Deane was never able to settle the matter. He was ruined financially and his reputation suffered from the dispute.

de Francy, Theveneau. See Francy, Theveneau de.

Denning, William. A New York businessman, he was active in state affairs during the Revolution. He was probably the man nominated by Fell on September 9, 1779, to a place on the Treasury Board. After the war he served in the New York Assembly and one term in the United States Congress, 1809-1810.

Delegate from New Jersey

Dickinson, John. A very important man in the deliberations leading to Independence, Dickinson is not very well-known today, possibly because of his conservative stance. He opposed Independence and hoped for conciliation to the end, even to the point of voting against the Declaration of Independence. However, after the break was made he was one of the staunchest supporters of Independence. In 1779 he was elected to the Continental Congress as a delegate from Delaware.

Drayton, William Henry. Coming from a prominent South Carolina family, he originally opposed resistance to Great Britain. However, he became a radical after being personally affected by what he considered the injustices of the colonial system. He occupied various positions in South Carolina and served in the Continental Congress from 1778 until his death in September 1779.

Duane, James. A New York lawyer, he served in the Continental Congress from 1774 to 1784. A conservative during the early stages of the Revolution, he tried to smooth out the differences between Great Britain and the colonies. As a member of Congress, he was a conservative figure whose major contributions were in connection with financial and Indian affairs. He assisted in the final draft of the Articles of Confederation. During 1781 attacks on his loyalty brought a spirited defense from some of the most distinguished members of Congress.

Dunlap, John. He was the official printer for Congress from 1778 to 1789. It was on his press that the Declaration of Independence was printed from Jefferson's manuscript, and the Constitution was first printed in his newspaper. Concentrating on book printing at first, Dunlap began, in 1771, the publication of a weekly newspaper, *The Pennsylvania Packet, or The General Advertiser.* In 1778 the paper was published three times a week, and in 1784 it became the first daily newspaper in the United States.

du Portail, Louis Lebeque, Chevalier. He was one of the French soldiers engaged by Benjamin Franklin and Silas Deane to serve in the American cause. He was first appointed colonel of engineers and later brigadier general. He was especially critical of British military leadership during the war.

Dyer, Eliphalet. A lawyer from Connecticut, he had a very active and constructive career prior to the outbreak of the Revolution. He served ably in the Continental Congress from 1774 to 1783. Apparently, he was not very popular personally, but most of his colleagues respected him for his ability.

Edwards, Evan. A major in the Eleventh Pennsylvania Regiment, he was transferred to the Fourth Regiment in January 1781.

Elbert, Samuel. He entered the Continental Army in 1776. He was taken prisoner at the Battle of Brier Creek in 1779. He later served as Governor of Georgia.

Ellery, William. A lawyer from Rhode Island, he sat in Congress from 1776 to 1786 with the exception of two years. His work for the Revolutionary cause was outstanding, beginning with service to Rhode Island and continuing in Congress. His special talent was in committee work. In 1777 and 1778 he served on at least fourteen committees, and in 1779 he was appointed to the newly-created Board of Admiralty.

Ellsworth, Oliver. A very successful Connecticut lawyer, he was one of the most able and active of American statesmen. He was connected with the Revolution almost from the beginning. He served in the Continental Congress for six years, beginning in 1777. In 1779 he was also appointed a member of the Council of Safety of Connecticut. He was later a member of the Constitutional Convention and Chief Justice of the United States Supreme Court in 1796.

Estaing, Charles Hector (Comte d'Estaing). A French soldier, he was very active in the Seven Years War with England. Named vice admiral of the French fleet, he was appointed commander of the fleet sent to aid the American colonies. He led the force that captured the West Indian islands of Grenada and St. Vincent. He returned to France in 1780.

Fell, Peter Renaudet. The son of John Fell, he served valiantly in the Revolution as lieutenant colonel of the militia. His service resulted in his disability from rheumatism. During the last two years of the war he was an aide to Governor Clinton of New York and was present at the taking of Stony Point. Following the war he attempted to continue in business, but his war-induced disability forced his retirement to his country estate. He died at Coldenham, New York, in 1789 at the age of thirty-seven.

Fleming, William. He was a delegate to Congress from Virginia from 1779 to 1781. A lawyer, he occupied many positions in Virginia before going to Congress, including seats in the House of Burgesses and the Committee of Independence. He continued to serve his state after the Revolution in various judicial positions.

Fleury, Louis de. He was one of the numerous Frenchmen who aided in the American cause. Commissioned by Congress, he served in several important battles, especially at Stony Point in 1779, for which he received a vote of thanks from Congress. In 1780 he left American service to join the French forces led by Rochambeau.

Flower, Benjamin. He was a lieutenant colonel and Commissary-General of Military Stores. Although Washington voiced confidence in him, he was not willing to promote him in May 1779 because of the many conflicting requests and demands for promotion.

Floyd, William. He was a member of the Continental Congress from New York from 1774 to 1777 and from 1778 to 1783. Never an outspoken or aggressive man, he played a minor role in the New York delegation. He was a very effective committeeman, and through diligent service he won the respect of his colleagues. He suffered very much in a financial way because of his support for the Revolutionary cause.

Fowler, Alexander. He was a British officer who later became Auditor of Accounts, Western Department of the Continental Army. He and other foreign officers created many problems for Washington and Congress in trying to assimilate them with as little difficulty as possible.

Francy, Theveneau de. A Frenchman, he was the agent of Beaumarchais in his attempts to secure payment from

Congress for the goods sent to America through Silas Deane before France became an ally. He was an able man who befriended financially the Marquis de Lafayette.

Franklin, Benjamin. One of the best known men in American history, he was the American minister to France in 1779. Previously he had shared the duties with Arthur Lee and Silas Deane, but this led to much trouble and confusion. Franklin was the man most responsible for the French alliance, and he was a very well-loved man in France.

Franks, David. A major in the Continental Army, he was an aide to Benedict Arnold at the time of his treason. Franks and other aides were acquitted of any complicity in the plot.

Frelinghuysen, Frederick. He was a New Jersey delegate to the Continental Congress in 1778, 1779, 1782, and 1783. He was one of the youngest members, being only twenty-five at his first election. He gave up a promising military career to serve in Congress, but after eight months of his first term he resigned, due mostly to restlessness. He later served in Congress again and in several positions in New Jersey.

Gambier, James. A career officer in the British navy, he was named rear admiral in 1778. He was second in command to Lord Howe in New York, but on occasion he acted as commander-in-chief.

Gansevoort, Peter. A Revolutionary soldier from New York, he was in command of Fort Schuyler at the time of the defeat of Burgoyne, an event in which he was a major participant. In 1779 he led an important raid against the Mohawks in New York. He remained a military officer during the remainder of his career.

Gates, Horatio. Born in England, he served in the British army until 1765, when he retired. He had been particularly active in the American phase of the Seven Years War in the course of which he became well acquainted with George Washington. On Washington's advice, he moved to Virginia in 1772 and became a prosperous planter. He was active in the Revolution from the beginning, but he was constantly embroiled in controversy, including disputes with General Schuyler, Benedict Arnold, and even with Washington himself. In 1778-1779 he was commander of the Eastern Department of the army, with headquarters in Boston.

Gerard de Rayneval, Conrad Alexandre. One of the secretaries of Vergennes, the Foreign Minister of France, he arranged and signed the alliance with the United States in 1778. He came the same year as the first accredited French minister to the United States and stayed until September 1779, when he was replaced by the Chevalier de la Luzerne. He was particularly important in deciding the terms of a treaty of peace with Britain and in establishing the boundaries to be claimed by the United States.

Gerry, Elbridge. A member of the Continental Congress from Massachusetts from 1776 to 1781 and 1782 to 1785, he had one of the most varied careers in the formative period of American history. A man of commercial interests, he was an early supporter of the cause of Independence. During his tenure in Congress, he offered especially good counsel on the Treasury Board. He later was a diplomat and Vice President of the United States.

Gibson, John. He was particularly active during and after the French and Indian War in obtaining and holding the area around Fort Pitt. During the Revolution he served in New York and New Jersey and commanded the Western Department after 1781.

Gist, Mordecai. A Revolutionary soldier from Maryland, he served ably, first in the state militia and later with the Continental Army. He was active in several major battles and was instrumental in protecting Maryland against British invasion.

Gravier, Charles (Comte de Vergennes). A French diplomat, he was the French Foreign Minister from 1774 to 1787. He signed the treaty with the United States in 1778 that brought France into the Revolution. He was the chief French negotiator in the Treaty of Paris, 1783.

Gray, George. He was a prominent Philadelphian who served on the Committee of Safety. From 1777 until the close of the war, he served on the Board of War, occasionally as President.

Grayson, William. He was a Revolutionary soldier commissioned lieutenant colonel and aide-de-camp to General Washington in 1776. He retired from the army in 1779 and later in the same year was appointed a commissioner of the Board of War. He served in the Continental Congress, 1785-1787.

Brief Biographies

Greene, Nathaniel. A Quaker from Rhode Island, he became one of the outstanding military leaders in the Revolution. As a major general, he was a close associate of General Washington, especially supporting him against those who wanted a new commander in chief. In February 1778 he became Quartermaster-General of the Continental Army. In this position, he reorganized the supply departments and helped alleviate much of the winter discomfort that troops had previously suffered.

Griffin, Cyrus. In the early days of the trouble with England, he advocated the colonial cause, but he also worked for reconciliation with Great Britain. He served in the Virginia legislature in 1777 and 1778, when he was elected to the Continental Congress (1778-1780). He was not particularly happy in Congress because of the bickering and delay. After holding various other state positions, he was returned to Congress, where he was the last president, beginning January 22, 1788, before the Constitution took effect.

Griffin, Samuel. A colonel in the Revolutionary War, he was wounded in the Battle of Harlem Heights in 1776. He later represented Virginia in Congress, 1789-1795.

Hamilton, James. A very capable British general, he was captured at the Battle of Saratoga. While imprisoned he concerned himself about the treatment of British prisoners of war.

Harnett, Cornelius. A delegate to the Continental Congress from 1777 to 1780, he had a very active career in the events leading to the Revolution. He has been called "the Samuel Adams of North Carolina." He rec-

Delegate from New Jersey

ommended that Independence be declared, and he was probably responsible for the provision in the first constitution of North Carolina forbidding an established church and guaranteeing religious freedom. He found Congressional service disagreeable and financially damaging. He also wearied of quarrels and jealousies of the other members. Captured by the British in 1781, he died while on parole.

Hart, John. A prominent leader of the Independence movement in New Jersey, he was elected to the Continental Congress in 1776, where he became a signer of th Declaration of Independence. When the British invaded New Jersey he was forced to hide in the forests, and his estate was destroyed.

Hartley, Thomas. An early supporter of the Revolutionary cause in Pennsylvania, he was commissioned lieutenant colonel by Congress in 1776 and distinguished himself at Germantown and Brandywine. His major military achievement was in his expedition in 1778 into Pennsylvania against the Indians. He received the commendation of Congress for this action. Beginning in 1779 he began a political career that took him into Congress for twelve years.

Harvie, John. In 1776 he was made a colonel of Virginia militia and distinguished himself, particularly in Indian affairs. In the same year Congress appointed him one of the commissioners for Indian affairs in the Middle Department. Elected to the Continental Congress in 1777, he served on the Board of War and on the Appeals, Marine, and Commerce committees. His most effective service was his appointment to a committee to reorganize the army and the department of supply in 1778. In 1778 he withdrew from Congress, finding service there disagreeable.

Heath, William. A farmer by occupation, he became a prominent military leader at the outbreak of the war. He served at Bunker Hill and eventually reached the rank of major general in the Continental Army. In 1777 he handled responsibilities so badly that he received a reprimand from Washington and was used for the remainder of the war mostly in staff duty.

Hele, Christopher. A lieutenant in the British navy, he was taken prisoner when his ship was wrecked in the Delaware River. Admiral Gambier protested his imprisonment as an infringement of the flag of truce. He often wrote to Congress protesting his imprisonment. He later broke his parole, although he informed Congress in advance that he intended to do so.

Henry, Patrick. Best known for his "liberty or death" speech, Henry was one of the most active radicals in Virginia in the pre-Independence period. He is said to have been as influential in Virginia as Samuel Adams was in Massachusetts. In 1776 he was elected Governor of Virginia and served until 1779, when he was succeeded by Thomas Jefferson. During Henry's administration he was faced with a British invasion of the state. He was instrumental in defeating the movement in 1778-1779 to remove George Washington as commander in chief.

Hewes, Joseph. An early leader in North Carolina for rebellion, he did not embrace Independence until John

Delegate from New Jersey

Adams convinced him of its popularity. He sat in the Continental Congress from 1774 to 1777 and in 1779 until his death that same year. His most distinguished service in Congress was in naval affairs; he has been considered in truth to be the first executive head of the United States Navy. He was an extremely popular man. One of the hardest working men in Congress, his cause of death has been diagnosed as a direct result of overwork.

Hill, Whitmel. He was a member of the Continental Congress from North Carolina from 1778 to 1781. He attained the rank of colonel in the army before going to Congress. He ably served his state in many positions before and after sitting in Congress.

Hogun, James. (Sometimes his name is spelled Hogan.) A member of the Provincial Congress of North Carolina, he served in various state military positions after the outbreak of hostilities. In 1779 he was appointed brigadier general.

Holker, John. He was the French consul to the United States. While here he became a partner of Robert Morris in private business. Finding it impossible to return home during the French Revolution, he married and moved to Virginia, where he spent the remainder of his life.

Holten, Samuel. He was a member of the Continental Congress from 1778 to 1780 and from 1782 to 1787. He was very active from the beginning of the Revolutionary movement, and he continued to serve Massachusetts and the United States until just before his death in

1816. In Congress he was interested in the western land claims and the Articles of Confederation. Because of his medical background, he performed ably on committees dealing with medical and surgical matters.

Hooper, Robert Lettice. A prominent New Jersey resident, he was appointed Deputy Quartermaster General in 1778. He came under question in 1779 for possibly diverting public equipment to private use. He was very active in trying to prevent trade with the enemy.

Hopkinson, Francis. A member of the Continental Congress from New Jersey, he was a signer of the Declaration of Independence and the designer of the American flag in 1777. From 1778 to 1781, while a member of Congress, he also held the office of Treasurer of Loans. A quarrel with the Treasury Board caused him to resign his position. A talented musician and poet, he was also a very active and able pamphleteer for the American cause.

Houston, William Churchill. Originally from North Carolina, he attended the College of New Jersey, where he became involved in local affairs. He served both as a member of the New Jersey Assembly and as deputy secretary of the Continental Congress. In 1779 he was elected a member of the Continental Congress, where he took a leading role in matters of finance and supply until his term ended in 1781.

Houstoun, John. One of the earliest Revolutionary leaders in Georgia, he attempted to bring that state in line with the others. This was most difficult, however, since royalist sentiment was very strong there. He was

Delegate from New Jersey

elected Governor of Georgia in 1778, but his administration was marred by the chaotic and unsuccessful attempt to drive the British out of St. Augustine, Florida.

Howe, Robert. A military man, he rose rapidly during the early phases of the Revolution. By 1777 he was a major general and in command of the Southern Department. An unpopular man, his orders to defend Savannah led to much local opposition. The necessity of evacuating the city in face of the British invasion resulted in a court-martial in which he was totally acquitted. He was later transferred to the North.

Howell, Joseph. He was paymaster to the Second Pennsylvania Regiment until his resignation in 1778. He later served as Commissioner of United States Army Accounts and acting Paymaster General until 1792.

Huntington, Jabez. A prominent leader in Connecticut, he became the major general over all the Connecticut militia in 1777, after having served in other civil and military offices. In February 1779 he was seized with a nervous disorder which ended his career and eventually brought on his death.

Huntington, Samuel. A prominent judicial and political leader of Connecticut, he held numerous state offices. He was also a member of the Continental Congress from 1775 until 1784. He had the double distinction of signing the Declaration of Independence and in September 1779, of being elected President of Congress. He later also served as Governor of Connecticut.

Irvine, William. A doctor by training, he became an officer in the Pennsylvania militia during the Revolution.

He was twice captured by the British, first in the unsuccessful Canadian invasion in 1776 and later at the Battle of Chestnut Hill, New Jersey in 1777. In 1779 he was made a brigadier general in the Continental Army.

Izard, Ralph. A wealthy South Carolina planter, Izard attempted to avoid conflict with England, but when Revolution came he staunchly supported Independence although he was no believer in democracy. In 1777 he was appointed by Congress as American minister to Tuscany, but he was never received by that government. He remained in France, where he became a bitter antagonist of Benjamin Franklin, who felt that Izard was trying to usurp his responsibilities in dealing with the French. He was recalled by Congress in 1779, but after explanations were received, Congress passed a resolution approving his conduct. He was also a friend of Arthur Lee and was involved in the Deane-Lee controversy. He later served in the United States Senate.

Jay, John. He was one of the most influential men in the formative period of the United States. Short of being President, he held virtually every other high office in the country. A conservative by nature and upbringing, he resisted the break with Great Britain, but once Independence came no one threw himself more wholly into the struggle. From 1776 to 1779 he was the Chief Justice of New York. In December 1778 he returned to the Continental Congress, having served there earlier, and he was shortly elected its president. He held that office until September 27, 1779, when he was elected Minister Plenipotentiary to Spain. His career included many diplomatic missions, and he was the first Chief Justice of the United States Supreme Court.

Delegate from New Jersey

Jennings, Edmund. A Virginian, he had long been interested in American rights before the Revolution. On September 29, 1779, he was nominated but not elected as a commissioner to examine the accounts of Silas Deane in France.

Johnson, Thomas. A member of the Continental Congress from Maryland and active in pre-Revolutionary incidents, he was at first hopeful of a reconciliation with Great Britain. In 1777 he raised a military force in Maryland and led it to Washington's headquarters in New Jersey. Elected in 1777, he was the first Governor of Maryland until 1779. He later served on the United States Supreme Court.

Kennedy, Sarah. She was the widow of Dr. Samuel Kennedy. Her husband had allowed the government to build a hospital on his farm in Pennsylvania. A dispute arose about the amount of land to be taken, the amount of government money spent, and the amount of damages to be claimed.

Knobelauch, Baron de. A lieutenant colonel, he was recruited for American military service in Paris by Benjamin Franklin and Arthur Lee. Upon arriving in America, he found there was no proper position for him, and over a period of time he was reduced to severe poverty. He appealed both to Washington and to Congress for aid.

Lafayette, Marquis de (Marie Joseph Paul Yves Roche Gilbert du Motier). He was one of the most popular and well-known foreign soldiers to participate in the American Revolution. As a volunteer in the Continental Army at his own expense, he served ably from 1777 to 1781. From 1778 to 1780 he was at home in France attempting to advance the American cause.

Langworthy, Edward. A Georgia delegate to the Continental Congress from 1777 to 1779, he played no conspicuous role in that body. He was a firm supporter of Washington in the attempts to supersede him, and he supported Silas Deane in his controversy with Arthur Lee. His actions in opposing the insistence on American fishing rights off Newfoundland caused Henry Laurens to point out that Langworthy's commission to sit in Congress had expired two months earlier. This ended his service in Congress.

Laurens, Henry. A prominent merchant and planter in South Carolina, he was an early leader in his state in the movement toward Independence. In 1777 he was sent to the Continental Congress, where he was unanimously elected its president on November 1. He became embroiled in several controversies, including attacks on Robert Morris, and sided with Arthur Lee in the Deane-Lee controversy. He was so upset by the actions of Congress relating to Deane that he resigned the presidency on December 9, 1778. He stayed in Congress until November 9, 1779, when he was elected to negotiate a treaty and a loan with the Dutch. He was captured on the way to Holland and for fourteen months was imprisoned in the Tower of London, where his treatment was severe.

Laurens, John. The son of Henry Laurens, he returned from Europe in 1777 to participate in the Revolution. He was at first a volunteer aide on Washington's staff and later was commissioned a lieutenant colonel. In 1778 he wounded General Charles Lee in a duel occasioned by Lee's attacks on Washington. He remained actively in the war until 1780, when he was named by Congress as Envoy Extraordinary to France to assist Franklin in military negotiations.

Lee, Arthur. A physician and lawyer with European training, he became involved as an agent of various American interests in Europe during the early stages of the Revolution. In 1776 he was appointed one of the three commissioners to negotiate a treaty with France. His associates, Benjamin Franklin and Silas Deane, were already hard at work in Paris when he arrived. His attempts to gain recognition from Spain and Prussia failed. He later began to attack Deane for his methods of acquiring supplies from France before a treaty was negotiated. He claimed that the supplies were intended as gifts, while Deane argued that they were to be paid for. The controversy bitterly divided Congress for months. In the long run, both men were recalled. Deane's career was destroyed despite the absence of proof against him. Lee continued to attack his enemies bitterly. He served in various positions, including the Continental Congress, until 1789.

Lee, Charles. He is one of the most difficult men in American history to judge. He came to the Revolution with a good reputation from the French and Indian War. However, his Revolutionary War service showed him to be little more than a soldier of fortune. While imprisoned by the British in 1777, he was suspected of treason, although the documents supporting this claim were not discovered until 1858. At the Battle of Monmouth, he retreated in face of the enemy. A court-martial judged him guilty of disobedience of orders, misbehavior before the enemy, and disrespect to the commander in chief. He was suspended from the army for twelve months. He attacked Washington so bitterly that Colonel John Laurens wounded him in a duel, preventing Anthony Wayne from challenging him. His attacks on Washington and Congress finally resulted in his dismissal from the army in 1780.

Lee, Richard Henry. A brother of Francis Lightfoot, William, and Arthur Lee, he was an early champion of opposition to Britain in Virginia. A close friend of Patrick Henry, Thomas Jefferson, and Samuel Adams, he led in the movement for Independence. His particular interest was in foreign affairs. Unfortunately, his vehement defense of his brother Arthur in the controversy with Silas Deane helped to divide Congress into two hostile camps. Exhausted from many years of service, he resigned from Congress in May 1779.

Lee, William. A brother of Richard Henry, Francis Lightfoot, and Arthur Lee, he was an American diplomat during the Revolution. Appointed by the secret committee of Congress as commercial agent at Nantes, he went to Paris, where he became deeply embroiled in the controversy between his brother Arthur and Silas Deane. In the midst of the controversy, Congress, acting without foresight, decided to appoint representatives to other European courts. William Lee was appointed to the courts of Berlin and Vienna. His attempts to secure recognition for the United States failed, and he was recalled in June 1779.

Lewis, Francis. A signer of the Declaration of Independence, he represented New York in the Continental Congress from 1775 to 1779. Afterwards, he served until 1781 on the Board of Admiralty. In Congress, Lewis seldom entered the debates, but he provided excellent service on the Marine, Secret, and Commercial committees. Since the Revolution cost him his fortune, he spent his declining years in the homes of his sons.

Lincoln, Benjamin. A moderately prosperous small-town farmer in Massachusetts, he became involved both politically and militarily during the Revolution. He was with the Massachusetts militia before his appointment as major general in the Continental Army. In 1778 after outstanding service in the North he was appointed commander of the Southern Department, where he immediately faced severe difficulties. In 1779 he and his whole army were captured at the fall of Charleston.

Livingston, Henry Brockholst. The son of Governor William Livingston of New Jersey, he entered the Continental Army as a captain and rose to lieutenant colonel by 1779. In that year he accompanied his brother-in-law John Jay to Spain as his private secretary.

Livingston, William. Beginning in New York and concluding in New Jersey, he had one of the most active careers of the era. After participating in New York affairs, he moved to New Jersey, where he was elected to the First and Second Continental Congresses. He was elected in 1776 as the first Governor of New Jersey, a post he held until his death fourteen years later. He served ably during one of the most trying times in the state's history.

Brief Biographies

Lopez, Aaron. He was a colonial merchant. Born in Portugal in 1731, in 1752 he arrived in Newport, Rhode Island, where he became active in the whale oil and candle trade. Despite much adversity, by the time of the Revolution he was a successful and prosperous merchant with complete or part ownership in at least thirty ships, but the war brought disruption and chaos to his business. He was one of the few Jews to attain prominence during the Revolution.

Lovell, James. A teacher by training and experience, Lovell was a rabid Revolutionary while his father became a Loyalist. He sat as a member of the Continental Congress from Massachusetts from 1777 to 1782. His service was marked by industry and zeal although he was extremely partisan. He belonged to the group that tried to displace General Washington, and he was one of the most severe opponents of Silas Deane. His major contribution, of which there were many despite his partisanship, was on the Committee on Foreign Affairs.

Lowndes, Rawlins. He was President of South Carolina from 1778 to 1779. A conservative by temperament and conviction, he had opposed the break with Britain but accepted the act when it came. As President he faced British invasion, poor health and the death of two sons, and open rebellion against his leadership. He was the last President of the state, his successor taking the title of Governor.

Loziers, ———. He, along with Brower, had been arrested by Sir Henry Clinton for killing a Loyalist named Richards. Washington protested the treatment of the two captives and requested that they be treated like any other prisoners of war.

Delegate from New Jersey

Luzerne, Anne Caesar de la. Originally a French soldier, he entered the diplomatic service in 1776. In 1779 he succeeded Gerard as the second minister to the United States. He stayed for four years and won the respect of most Americans through his friendship, wisdom, and prudence.

McComb, John. Born in New Jersey, before the Revolution he lived in New York, where he was an architect and builder. In 1777 he moved to Princeton, where he was made a quartermaster in the Continental Army.

McIntosh, Lachlan. At the outbreak of the Revolution he became a colonel of the Georgia militia and later was commissioned brigadier general in the Continental Army. After several problems of personality with other officers, he was appointed commander of the Western Department at Fort Pitt. His subordinates, Daniel Brodhead and George Morgan, complained of his conduct and were successful in having him removed in March 1779. He was then reassigned to the South, where he attempted to take Savannah. He was captured by the British in the fall of Charleston in 1780.

McKean, Thomas. He was one of the most active radicals in the Pennsylvania-Delaware area before the Revolution and a signer of the Declaration of Independence. Because of the uncertain status of Delaware, he was able to hold office in both that state and Pennsylvania at the same time. From 1778 to 1783 he served in the Continental Congress, where he was associated with the Lee faction in the Deane-Lee dispute. He was a fierce critic of inefficiency, corruption, and militarism.

Brief Biographies

McNeil, Hector. An officer in the Continental Navy, he was third on the list of captains. He served ably until 1777, when his ship, the *Boston,* escaped from a battle with three English vessels. The American ships were separated in the battle and McNeil was lucky to escape. Nonetheless, he was court-martialed and suspended from the navy in 1778. Despite the recommendation of the Marine Committee that the sentence not be carried out, McNeil never again served in the navy.

McNutt, Alexander. Long a promoter of colonization in Nova Scotia, he attempted to foment rebellion there in conjunction with the American Revolution. He advocated invasion from the United States and finally got a grant from Congress to open a road into the area. His plans were too ambitious to be carried out successfully.

McPherson, William. An American sailor in the British navy, he resigned his commission at the outbreak of the Revolution, but it was not accepted until 1779. At this time he joined the American army with the rank of brevet major and served as aide-de-camp to Lafayette. He later had a command of his own.

Marchant, Henry. An active leader in the Revolutionary movement in Rhode Island, from 1777 to 1779 he was a delegate to the Continental Congress, where he served on the Marine, Appeals, Treasury, and Southern Department committees. He was later elected to Congress in 1780, 1783, and 1784, but he did not sit.

Mason, David. A colonel of engineers, he was prominent in military activity before his assignment to the ordnance works at Springfield, Massachusetts.

Delegate from New Jersey

Maxwell, William. A soldier with valuable experience in the French and Indian War, he was a very competent brigadier general in the Revolution. After serving under Washington in several major expeditions, he accompanied General Sullivan in an expedition against the Indians of the Six Nations in Western Pennsylvania and New York.

Mifflin, Thomas. A delegate from Pennsylvania to the First Continental Congress, he was one of youngest and most radical members. With the outbreak of war he entered the military. Rising to the position of Quartermaster General, he faced much criticism of his activities and became actively involved in the plot to replace Washington with General Gates. Despite the insistence of Congress that he continue in military service, he resigned his commission on February 25, 1779, and became active in state politics.

Montfort, Julius de. One of the many French volunteers, he was a major in Pulaski's regiment.

Morgan, Daniel. A Virginian by adoption, he was one of the most loyal and valuable officers under Washington's command. He took part in numerous important battles. He resigned his commission in 1779 because of poor health and dissatisfaction with the promotion policy of Congress. He later returned to active service and was instrumental in several crucial battles in the South.

Morgan, George. A native of Pennsylvania, he served both as Indian agent in the Middle Department and Deputy Commissary General of Purchases for the Western District, with headquarters at Fort Pitt. After about three years service, he resigned in 1779. He was also involved as a speculator in the controversy over the Indiana claims. This area, in the present state of West Virginia just south of the Pennsylvania line, was contested by Morgan's company and the state of Viriginia, which claimed jurisdiction. Morgan was never able to press his claim.

Morgan, John. He was the Director General and Physician in Chief in the general hospitals of the army until he was removed in 1777. He demanded an inquiry into his conduct, and the report, which acquitted him of any wrongdoing, was accepted by Congress in 1779. Rather than being condemned, he was commended for his service.

Morris, Gouverneur. A young man in his twenties during the Revolution, he was nevertheless among the most influential political leaders. Originally a conservative, he joined the Independence movement with great fervor despite the personal sacrifice involved. He was a nationalist before there was a national government, and he strongly defended the Continental Congress from all attacks. He was a delegate to Congress from New York in 1778-1779. A very capable member, he was most interested in financial, military, and diplomatic matters. In 1779 he was defeated for re-election primarily because he would not support New York's claim to Vermont. He then moved to Pennsylvania, where he continued his valuable service to the nation.

Morris, Robert. He was the first Chief Justice of New Jersey, holding the post from 1777 to 1779. Although his term was short his accomplishments were major because it fell to him to formulate rules for the high court and to organize the state judicial system.

Morris, Robert. He was one of the leading financiers of the Revolution. Hesitant at first to support Independence, he later became one of its major supporters. Because of his partnership in one of Philadelphia's leading mercantile houses he became deeply involved in the purchase of supplies and as a banker for the colonies. In 1779 he was charged by Thomas Paine and Henry Laurens with conducting private business while in public office and with involvement in fraudulent transactions. Although he was completely acquitted of any wrongdoing, his popularity declined significantly, possibly because of his great wealth and the fact that he never hesitated to make profit or take his commission when acting for the government.

Moultrie, William. A leading citizen of South Carolina, he served in state forces before his commission as a brigadier general in the Continental Army. His ability was not questioned, but he was criticized for negligence and loose command. His major military achievement came in 1779, when he saved Charleston from British capture. He was later Governor of the state.

Muhlenberg, John Peter Gabriel. A Lutheran clergyman, he served a church in Virginia at the outbreak of the Revolution. He exchanged his clerical garb for a military uniform and distinguished himself in several engagements, including his support of Anthony Wayne at Stony Point. He was commissioned a brigadier general in 1777 and was brevetted major general in 1783.

Brief Biographies

Mumford, Thomas. He was a merchant who had contracted in 1778 with Colonel Wadsworth, Commissary General of Purchases, to buy flour for the use of the army in Rhode Island.

Neilson, John. A New Jersey merchant, he raised a company of state militia and rose to the rank of brigadier general. On two occasions—1776 and 1778—he was elected to the Continental Congress but, believing he could provide better service in the military, refused to sit.

Nelson, Thomas. A signer of the Declaration of Independence and later Governor of Virginia, he sat in the Continental Congress in 1779. However, ill health forced him to return home, where he served in various capacities. An ardent Revolutionary, he can in no way be considered a radical.

Paca, William. Associated with most of the important political movements during his lifetime, he was one of the most influential men in Maryland. He signed the Declaration of Independence and was governor, judge, and member of the ratification convention for the Constitution. From 1775 to 1779 he served almost without interruption in Congress, where he was especially valuable on the Committee on Foreign Affairs.

Paine, Thomas. Best known as a pamphleteer and agitator, he was very influential in the events leading to Revolution. As a reward, he was appointed by Congress in 1777 as secretary to the Committee on Foreign Affairs. He served ably here until he became embroiled in the Deane-Lee controversy. He backed Arthur Lee, who claimed that French goods sent through Beaumarchais were meant as gifts to the United States. Deane, who had made the arrangements, claimed that they were purchases. The issue became a public one in the newspapers. In one of his articles, Paine revealed confidential information that he had access to because of his position, and he implied that France was aiding the colonies before the formal alliance was signed. For his indiscretion, he resigned under pressure on January 8, 1779. In November he was appointed as a clerk of the Pennsylvania Assembly.

Peabody, Nathaniel. He was a member of the Continental Congress from New Hampshire from 1779 to 1780. With a medical background, he performed ably on the Medical Committee and on a special committee to investigate the dangerous military condition in 1780. After leaving the Continental Congress in 1780, he continued to serve his state in various capacities.

Penet, Peter. He was a member of the firm of Penet, Windel & Co., manufacturers of arms—muskets, bayonets, and ammunition.

Pettit, Charles. A prominent public servant of New Jersey, he was appointed in 1778 at the insistence of General Nathaniel Greene as Assistant Quartermaster-General of the Continental Army. He was assigned to keep the accounts and cash, a duty he ably performed by introducing much needed reforms. He remained in this position until 1781.

Phillips, William. A British soldier with a good record in the Seven Years War, he was commissioned major general in America only in 1776. He served in several important engagements prior to being captured by the Americans at the Battle of Saratoga. After Burgoyne's return to England, the command of the Convention Troops fell to him. In 1779 he was allowed to go on parole to New York, where he lived until he was exchanged for General Benjamin Lincoln in 1780.

Pinckney, Thomas. One of the most successful of early American diplomats, he started his public career as a soldier during the Revolutionary War. He was involved mostly in the campaigns in the South; he was made a special aide to Count d'Estaing at Savannah primarily because of his knowledge of French. He later served as Governor of South Carolina and as minister to Great Britain and Spain.

Plater, George. Active in Maryland affairs as the Revolution approached, he was elected to the Continental Congress, where he served from 1778 to 1780. He later presided over the ratification convention for the Constitution and served as Governor of the state.

Potter, James. An early leader in the Revolutionary movement in Pennsylvania, he was chosen colonel of a battalion of militia in 1776. He served well but resigned in 1778 for personal reasons. Washington tried to induce him to return to duty in 1779. He was mostly concerned with Indian activities in 1779–1780.

Potts, Jonathan. A friend and relative of the famous doctor, Benjamin Rush, he was the first graduate of the medical school of the College of Philadelphia, now the University of Pennsylvania. In the early part of the

Revolution when he was ministering to Pennsylvania troops, he was taken into Continental service by Congress and sent north with General Gates. In 1778 he was appointed Deputy Director General of the hospitals in the Middle Department.

Prescott, William. He was charged directly with fortifying Bunker Hill but chose instead to defend Breed's Hill. He was active in the surrender of General Burgoyne in 1777, but an early injury kept him from further active military service. He continued in various civil positions until his death.

Prevost, Augustine. A British soldier, he served in the southern states where he won several battles. In 1779 he prevented the capture of Charleston and Savannah by American forces.

Pulaski, Casimir. He was one of the many outstanding foreign soldiers to aid substantially in the American Revolution. He fought foreign domination of his native Poland. After coming to Boston in 1776 he served as a volunteer in several capacities. In 1778 Congress commissioned him to organize a cavalry corps, and in 1779 he was sent to support General Lincoln in South Carolina. He died from wounds suffered in the Battle of Charleston in 1779.

Putnam, Israel. Very well known for his military service at the Battle of Bunker Hill, his most constructive service was made in the events leading to Revolution. He was commissioned a major general in the Continental Army, but he was a serious problem for Washington because he often disobeyed orders. His excessive self-confidence hindered what might have been a very illustrious military career. His duty was ended in December 1779 by a paralytic stroke.

Rawlings, Moses. He was a prominent Maryland planter. During the Revolution he became a capable officer, eventually reaching the rank of lieutenant colonel and receiving very warm praise from Washington. Rawlings was captured at the Battle of Fort Washington.

Read, Thomas. A captain in the United States Navy, he had previously commanded the brigantine *Baltimore*. He was appointed by the Marine Committee on September 30, 1779, to command the frigate *Bourbon*.

Reed, Joseph. A distinguished lawyer, soldier, and member of the Continental Congress, he was elected President of the Supreme Executive Council of Pennsylvania, serving from 1778 to 1781. His administration was a very crucial one. Slavery was abolished in Pennsylvania and Pennsylvania soldiers were placed on half-pay for life. He was particularly aggressive in the prosecution of Benedict Arnold for his actions while in command of Philadelphia and in upholding the state's rights before Congress.

Riedesel, Baron Friedrich Adolph. A native of Brunswick with a good reputation in the Seven Years War, he was among the Germans hired by the British to fight in the American Revolution. As major general, he commanded the 4,000 Brunswick soldiers. A capable officer whose advice was not followed, he was captured at the Battle of Saratoga in 1777 and remained a prisoner until his exchange in 1779. He was then given a command

Delegate from New Jersey

on Long Island with headquarters at the present Brooklyn Heights.

Rivington, James. A printer who published the *New York Gazetteer,* he took a Loyalist position and often found himself in deep trouble with the American revolutionaries. On at least one occasion his printing plant was destroyed by the Sons of Liberty.

Roberdeau, Daniel. A prominent merchant in Philadelphia, he served in several capacities on the local level before the Revolution. He was extremely popular with the public. While in Congress from 1777 to 1779 he was among the strongest advocates of honesty, efficiency, an adequate army, and a sound currency. He denounced war profiteers in a fiery speech in 1779.

Root, Jesse. A minister by training, he abandoned the pulpit after a short time and became a lawyer in Connecticut. At the outbreak of the Revolution, he joined the state forces, rising to adjutant general. He rendered valuable service in the Continental Congress from 1778 to 1782.

Ross, John. A prominent merchant in Philadelphia, he aided the patriot cause in the early days of the Revolution. In 1776 he was employed by the Commercial Committee to purchase supplies for the army. His contracts required that he establish agencies in Nantes and Paris, and he made several trips to France himself. During the course of the war he spent £20,000 more than he was ever repaid by Congress.

Rutgers, Henry. A very important citizen of New York, he served in the military during the Revolution. Little

Brief Biographies

is known about his army career except that he served as a captain at the Battle of White Plains and was a muster master. In 1795 he resigned from the New York militia to devote time to his many other interests.

Rutledge, John. An aristocrat from South Carolina, he was a conservative and distrustful of democracy. He tried to avoid an open break with Britain, but when it came he joined with fervor in the Revolutionary struggle. He served as President (Governor) of the state from 1776 to 1778 and again in 1779, at the critical point when invasion was threatened. He made valiant efforts to protect the state, but his actions resulted in questions which have not been fully answered even yet being raised as to his purposes.

St. Clair, Arthur. A resident of Westmoreland County, Pennsylvania, he tried to extend Pennsylvania control over the Pittsburgh area, putting him in conflict with Virginia officials. During the Revolution he served as a colonel in the retreat from Canada. In 1777 he was ordered to defend Fort Ticonderoga, then considered impregnable. His evacuation led to his recall by Congress and a court-martial trial, which exonerated him. He was not used, however, in any significant way for the rest of the war.

Schuyler, Philip John. A member of a very important New York family, he was one of the first four major generals commissioned by Congress to serve under Washington and was given command of the Northern Department. He antagonized the New Englanders and developed a running feud with General Gates. After the Battle of Saratoga, rumors circulated that he was incompetent and disloyal. A trial by court-martial held at his insistence in 1778 resulted in acquittal. In the spring of 1779 he resigned from the army but remained prominent in public life until 1798.

Scudder, Nathaniel. He was a New Jersey doctor and a member of the Continental Congress from 1777 to 1779. He was frequently absent from Congress on travel necessitated by his membership on the Committee on the Quartermaster Corps. He is believed to be the one most responsible for convincing the New Jersey legislature to ratify the Articles of Confederation.

Searle, James. From being a successful merchant in Philadelphia he went on to a very valuable public career. After serving in local positions, he was elected in 1778 to the Continental Congress, where he served on the Marine, Commerce, and Foreign Affairs Committees. He was a supporter of Arthur Lee in his dispute with Silas Deane. He was nominated as secretary to the embassy in Spain in 1779, but his name was withdrawn. In 1780 he became a special foreign envoy for Pennsylvania.

Sherman, Roger. After a rather inauspicious beginning, Sherman became one of the most influential men in the country. A member of the Continental Congress from Connecticut from 1774 to 1781 and again in 1783-1784, he had more legislative experience than any other member. Although belonging to the conservative wing of the Revolutionary Party, he may well have been, toward the end of the Revolution, the most influential member of Congress.

Brief Biographies

Shippen, William. A very successful physician in Philadelphia, he served the Continental Army during the Revolution. In 1777 he was appointed Chief Physician and Director General of Hospitals. Probably it was his plan for the reorganization of the army medical department that brought him to the attention of Congress and secured him the appointment. A court-martial trial for alleged financial irregularity ended in his being acquitted, and he served in his position until 1781.

Smith, James. A member of the Continental Congress from Pennsylvania and a signer of the Declaration of Independence, he was one of the most ardent defenders of the rights of the back-country counties in their protests against eastern control of the states. He was not a well known member of Congress and was regarded as something of an eccentric.

Smith, Jonathan Bayard. He was an ardent member of the Revolutionary Party in Philadelphia. He was very active in military affairs in Pennsylvania and even resigned his election to Congress in 1777 to aid in the defense of Philadelphia. He was again elected to Congress in December 1777 and served the following year. He was a member of the Board of War and of the committee to supervise publication of the journals of Congress.

Spencer, Joseph. A prominent resident of Connecticut, he served the state well militarily in the early stages of the Independence movement. However, in resentment at the commissioning of Israel Putnam, his subordinate in Connecticut, to a higher rank in the Continental Army than his own, he left the army without notice. Eventually, he was reconciled and later was promoted to major general. Further controversy caused his resignation from the army in 1778. He was elected to the Continental Congress in 1779.

Steuben, Friedrich Wilhelm Ludolf Gerhard Augustin (Baron von Steuben). He may well have been the single most important foreign military officer in the American Revolution. After distinguished service in the Prussian army, he came to America through the encouragement of Beaumarchais, Franklin, and Deane and was assigned to Washington's staff. Here he so successfully undertook the training of the army that the Continentals were equal to the British regulars in discipline and skill. In 1779 he was named Inspector General, and during the winter of 1779-1780 he was Washington's representative to the Continental Congress in efforts to reorganize the army.

Stirling, Sir Thomas. One of the first British officers to be sent at the outbreak of the Revolution, he was advanced from major to lieutenant colonel for his participation in several important battles. In 1779 he was made aide-de-camp to the King and colonel in the army.

Stirling, William, Earl of. His real name was William Alexander, but he is better known as Lord Stirling because of his claim to a Scottish peerage. In the Revolution, he was a major general with a close acquaintance with General Washington. He supported Washington against the so-called "Conway Cabal," the attempt to replace him with General Gates.

Sullivan, John. After serving in both the First and Second Continental Congresses he was commissioned a major general in the Continental Army in 1776. Because of controversies concerning his military skill he was often the subject of dispute in Congress. In 1779 he led an expedition into western Pennsylvania and New York against the Indians. He was very successful, but his health suffered so much that he resigned his commission on November 30, 1779.

Sumner, Jethro. A modestly prominent and prosperous resident of North Carolina, he became actively involved in the state militia during the Revolution. In January 1779 he was elected a brigadier general of the Continental Army. He was very active in recruiting North Carolina battalions.

Temple, John. He came from England in 1776 with money furnished him by the government. His mission was never clear, but he did anger Loyalists by his American sympathies.

Thompson, William. A capable military officer from Pennsylvania, he was ordered to participate in the invasion of Canada in 1776. Taken prisoner, he was finally exchanged in 1780. While on parole he bitterly attacked Thomas McKean, a member of Congress from Pennsylvania, for allegedly hindering his exchange. Congress responded by voting Thompson guilty of an insult to its honor and dignity and a breach of privilege. After Thompson was summoned before Congress for an apology, McKean won a judgment of £5,700 from him in a lawsuit.

Thomson, Charles. An orphaned Irish immigrant, he was fortunate enough to receive a good education and moved successively from teacher to businessman to politician. For his great activity in the Independence movement in Pennsylvania, John Adams called him "the Sam Adams of Philadelphia." Although the conservative Joseph Galloway prevented Thomson's election to the Continental Congress, he was chosen its secretary and held the position for the entire fifteen-year life of that body.

Trent, William. An Indian trader and land speculator, he was prominent in the Fort Duquesne-Fort Pitt area during the French and Indian War. In 1768 he, George Morgan, and others acquired a grant of land known as "Indiana" from the Indians on the upper Ohio. The land grant, which was denied British confirmation, was merged with Vandalia, a larger area. In 1779, after failing to get Virginia's approval, Trent vainly appealed to Congress for confirmation of the title. He continued to press his claim until 1783, but with no success.

Trumbull, John. The "painter of the Revolution," he had a military career until 1777, when he resigned his commission. Most of the time he served as aide-de-camp to various generals. In 1780 he went to Europe to study painting.

Trumbull, Jonathan. A successful merchant in Connecticut, he occupied many state political positions and was Governor from 1769 to 1784. He was the only colonial governor to join the radical side in the Revolution. Relatively free from conflict, Connecticut became a major supplier for the Continental Army. In supervising this work Trumbull made his greatest contribution to the cause. Although sometimes at odds with Trumbull,

Brief Biographies

Washington readily acknowledged that without his work the Continental Army would have been hard pressed for survival.

Trumbull, Jonathan (Jr.). A member of a well-known Connecticut family, he served in several important state offices both before and after the Revolution. In 1775 he was appointed paymaster of the New York Department of the Continental Army, a post he held until 1778, when he resigned to undertake the settlement of the accounts of his recently deceased brother, Commissary General Joseph Trumbull. He was also elected by Congress as Comptroller of the Treasury and Commissioner of the Board of Treasury. After the Revolution he was a Governor of Connecticut.

Trumbull, Joseph. Although he had mostly a business and political background, his service as Commissary General of the Connecticut troops convinced Washington to urge his appointment to the same position for the Continental forces. Serving from 1775 to 1778, he did an admirable job of organizing and operating the feeding of the army. Despite occasional complaints he was judged quite competent. He died in 1778 from illness resulting directly from his service to the Patriot cause.

Van Cortland, Philip. A soldier in New York in the early stages of the Revolution, he was active throughout the conflict, serving with particular distinction in the campaign that resulted in the surrender of Cornwallis at Yorktown in 1781. He was a member of the court-martial that heard charges against Benedict Arnold pressed by Pennsylvania authorities in 1778.

Van Schaick, Goose. (His given name was often spelled Gosen or Goosen.) He spent most of his life as a soldier, making his greatest contribution during the Revolution. During the war he became a colonel and saw much service on the northern and western frontiers of New York. The troops under his command were especially known for their excellent discipline. His greatest exploit came in April 1779, when he led a detachment against the Onondaga Indians. He took thirty-two prisoners, killed several Indians, burned towns, and destroyed stores and supplies, all without the loss of a man.

Varick, Richard. A New York soldier, he served first as military secretary to General Philip Schuyler and then as Deputy Commissary General of Musters. An aide to Benedict Arnold, he was horrified at his treason. Although a court of inquiry which Varick requested acquitted him of any involvement, suspicion lingered until Washington displayed extreme confidence by choosing him to copy and arrange all the correspondence and records of the Continental Army.

Vergennes, Comte de. See Gravier, Charles.

Von Steuben, Baron. See Steuben.

Wadsworth, Jeremiah. At the outbreak of the Revolution he was appointed commissary to the Revolutionary forces in Connecticut. His success here and his knowledge of mercantile affairs caused Congress to elect him Deputy Commissary General of Purchases in 1777 and Commissary General in 1778. His ability made possible the provisioning of the Continental Army despite lack of money and cooperation from state authorities.

Brief Biographies

Washington, George. He was commander in chief of the Continental Army and later first President of the United States. During 1778-1779 he had to deal with a Congress reluctant to move decisively, thinking that the French alliance would solve the war's problems. Washington often found it necessary to attend Congress, where he used his considerable influence to move the body to action.

Waterbury, David. A brigadier general of Connecticut forces, he served in various campaigns in New England. He was captured at the Battle of Valcour Bay in 1776 but was quickly exchanged. He remained in active service for the remainder of the war.

Wayne, Anthony. Active in the Revolution from the beginning, he served with Washington in various campaigns and wintered with him at Valley Forge. In July 1779 he surprised the British at their most northern post on the Hudson, Stony Point, where he took over 500 prisoners and valuable supplies. Congress was so pleased by this victory that it ordered a special medal to be presented to him.

Webb, Samuel Blatchley. Private secretary and aide-de-camp to General Washington in the early stages of the Revolution, he organized the 3rd Connecticut Regiment and took command of it in 1777. He was captured at the Battle of Long Island in December 1777 and remained a prisoner unil his exchange in 1780. He continued active military service after the release.

Whipple, William. A signer of the Declaration of Independence, he represented New Hampshire in Congress from 1776 to 1779. Because of his shipping and mercantile experience, he was especially critical of the defects in the navy and the inefficiency in public service. He was very much concerned about speculators and Loyalists.

Whiting, William. He was an expert cannon maker from Connecticut who was consulted about the possibility of Congress taking over the Salisbury furnace to manufacture ordnance.

Wilkinson, James. He is best known for his association with Aaron Burr and the conspiracy in the Southwest during Jefferson's Administration, but his career began during the Revolution. He served with Generals Gates, Arnold, and Washington. In 1778 he was named secretary to the newly-created Board of War. In 1779 he was appointed Clothier General but was forced to resign in 1781 because of irregularities in his accounts.

Willing, James. He was an American captain held prisoner by the British. According to Washington he was held by the British in retaliation for the confinement of Governor Hamilton in Virginia. Washington expressed his hope in September 1779 that both men could soon be released.

Witherspoon, John. A prominent Presbyterian minister in Scotland, he came to New Jersey in 1768 as president of the College of New Jersey (Princeton). A signer of the Declaration of Independence, he served with brief interruptions in the Continental Congress from 1776 to 1782. A very important member, he sat on over 100 committees, including he Board of War and the secret Committee on Foreign Affairs.

Brief Biographies

Yeates, Jasper. A lawyer from Pennsylvania, he was a moderate supporter of Independence after it became obvious that reconciliation was impossible. He saw little military service because he was commissioned by Congress to negotiate a treaty with the Indians at Fort Pitt. He was not, apparently, a Muster Master as Fell's diary entry on April 1 would suggest.

Zedwitz, Herman Baron. (Sometimes the name is spelled Zedtwitz in the *Journals*.) He was a German soldier serving in the Continental Army with the rank of lieutenant colonel. For traitorous acts he was sentenced to prison for the duration of the war. However, on July 14, 1779, after three years confinement, he was released on parole because of health and family reasons and deported.

BIBLIOGRAPHICAL NOTE

The editorial work involved in making Fell's diary meaningful required the use of some of the basic primary and secondary source material on this period. The information in the notes on the daily diary entries and the biographical material came from the works listed below, and those footnoted in the biography of Fell.

Burnett, Edmund Cody. *The Continental Congress.* New York, 1941, paperbound edition, 1964.

―――― (ed.). *Letters of Members of the Continental Congress.* 7 vols. Washington, 1921-1934.

Fitzpatrick, John C. (ed.). *The Writings of George Washington.* 39 vols. Washington, 1931-1944.

Ford, Worthington Chauncey, *et al.* (eds.). *Journals of the Continental Congress 1774-1789.* 34 vols. Washington, 1904-1937. (Cited as *Journal*[s])

Johnson, Allen, and Dumas Malone, (eds.). *Dictionary of American Biography.* 20 vols. New York, 1928-1936.

Lossing, Benson John (ed.). *Harper's Encyclopaedia of United States History.* 10 vols. New York, 1906.

U. S. Congress. *Biographical Directory of the American Congress 1774-1961.* Washington, 1961.

Who Was Who in America. Chicago, 1963.

Wilson, James Grant, and John Fiske (eds.). *Appleton's Cyclopaedia of American Biography.* 6 vols. New York, 1888-1889.

Winsor, Justin (ed.). *Narrative and Critical History of America.* 8 vols. Boston, 1889.

INDEX

Adams, John, 78, 131, 132-133, 141, 152, 161, 171-172, 198
Adams, Samuel, 18, 30, 47, 49, 64, 75, 76, 152, 171, 179, 198
Adams, Thomas, 28, 33, 152-153
Aitken, Robert, 63-64, 153
Albouy, Capt., 76
Alexander, William, 196
Alison, John, 94, 153
Allen, Ethan, 106, 153
Armand, Charles Treflin, Marquis de la Rouaire, 41, 42, 153
Armstrong, John, 76, 105, 113, 154
Arnold, Benedict, 10, 37-38, 40, 46, 53, 58-59, 62-63, 68-69, 72-73, 79, 80, 134-135, 153, 154, 159, 166, 167, 191, 199, 200, 202
Articles of Confederation, 130-131, 152, 157, 162, 173, 194

Ashmead, John, 101, 154
Atlee, Samuel John, 21, 24, 25, 47, 94, 154

Baylor, George, 84, 155
Beatty, John, 28-29, 35, 148, 155
Beaumarchais, Pierre Augustin Caron de, 32, 54, 86-87, 88, 155, 161, 165, 188, 196
Bedlow, William, 36, 37, 43, 155-156
Bingham, William, 41, 50, 89, 120, 156
Bland, Theodorick, 72, 84, 156
Brackenridge, Hugh Henry, 109, 156
Bradford, William, Jr., 33, 66, 156-157
Bretigny, Marquis de, 35, 38, 157
Brodhead, Daniel, 138, 157, 182
Brower, ———, 22, 157, 181
Brownrigg, Lt., 27
Burgoyne, John, 166, 189, 190

Index

Burke, Thomas, 17, 22, 24, 31, 34, 37, 47, 51, 52, 56, 104, 108, 157
Burnett, Edmund C., 136
Burr, Aaron, 202

Calwalader, Lambert, 35, 157-158
Caldwell, Samuel, 111
Cambray, Chevalier de, 39, 40
Camp, Caleb, 116, 158
Campbell, Sir Archibald, 38, 158
Carmichael, William, 51, 53, 75, 88, 133, 158
Celeron, Lewis, 44, 49-50, 158
Clark, Abraham, 21, 159
Clarke, Elijah, 29, 94, 159
Clarkson, Matthew, 40, 44, 51, 60-61, 159
Clinton, George, 31, 39, 46, 74, 159, 164
Clinton, Sir Henry, 22, 157, 159-160, 181
Clinton, James, 87
Clothing department, 48, 59, 62, 66-67, 69, 105, 106, 111-112, 114, 115, 117, 129
Colden, Cadwallader, 7
Collins, John, 49, 160
Condict, Silas, 94, 160
Conyngham, Gustavus, 114-115, 160
Cornwallis, Lord, 199
Cox, John, 103, 108, 110, 160
Cunningham, Joseph, 22, 116
Currency, 16-17, 41, 48, 53, 67, 81, 108, 126
Curson, R., 45
Curson, Samuel, 19

Dana, Francis, 133, 160-161
Davies, Col., 87
Deane-Lee controversy, 10, 15, 23, 25, 27, 30, 34, 69, 79, 96, 100, 114, 127, 131-132, 152, 155, 161, 175, 177, 182, 187-188
Deane, Silas, 15, 19, 20, 23, 25, 27, 34, 58, 68, 69, 74, 78, 79, 95, 96, 114, 121-122, 131, 134, 155, 158, 161, 163, 166, 176, 177, 178, 179, 181, 188, 194, 196
de Francy, Theveneau, *see* Francy, Theveneau de
Denning, William, 128-129, 147, 150, 161
Dereville, Pierre, 89
Dickinson, John, 76-77, 88, 94, 95, 105, 112, 117, 129, 162
Dodge, ———, 94
Donnell, John, 24
Drayton, William Henry, 24, 25, 81-82, 94, 104, 127, 162
Duane, James, 17, 18, 20, 22, 30, 34, 47, 53, 104, 105, 108, 162
Duarti, ———, 113, 116
Dunlap, John, 27, 162-163
du Portail, Louis Lebeque, Chevalier, 19, 28, 34, 39, 88, 163
Dyer, Eliphalet, 31, 36, 40, 47, 49, 51, 56, 163

Edwards, Evan, 66-67, 163
Elbert, Samuel, 67, 163
Ellery, William, 25, 33, 34, 40, 74, 75, 163-164
Ellsworth, Oliver, 17, 19, 33, 34, 164
Esdale, Gen., 94
Estaing, Charles Hector (Comte d'Estaing), 35, 38, 42-43, 87, 89, 137, 146-147, 164, 189
Ewing, George, 78

207

Fell, Elizabeth, 6
Fell, John, 18, 22, 24, 31, 34, 51, 74, 75, 77, 78, 79, 82, 83, 85, 87, 90, 92, 93, 99, 100, 104, 108, 109, 111, 116, 117, 119, 120, 122, 123, 124, 125, 126, 127, 129, 131, 135, 136, 137, 139, 146, 150, 161; biography, 6-11; early life, 6-7; revolutionary activity, 7-8; taken prisoner, 8; elected to Continental Congress, 9; death, 9; character and personality, 9-11
Fell, Peter Renaudet, 6, 7, 14, 97, 103, 105, 106, 112, 115, 164
Fell, Susanna, 97, 103
Fell, Symon, 6
Fishery question, 10, 60, 65, 85-86, 97, 98, 105-106, 108, 109-110, 114-115, 117, 119, 120, 177
Fleming, William, 104, 164-165
Fleury, Louis de, 25, 26, 68, 165
Flower, Benjamin, 36, 37, 44-45, 74, 165
Floyd, William, 37, 40, 165
Foreman, Ezekiel, 146
"Fort Wilson Riot," 135
Fowler, Alexander, 33, 50, 165
Francy, Theveneau de, 32, 86-87, 88, 165-166
Franklin, Benjamin, 75, 76, 78, 93, 123, 132, 133, 152, 161, 163, 166, 175, 176, 178, 196
Franks, David, 38, 166
Frazer, Perzifor, 112, 114, 115
Frelinghuysen, Frederick, 9, 35, 36, 51, 53, 57, 62, 166

Galloway, Joseph, 198
Gambier, James, 30, 56, 58, 166, 171
Gansevoort, Peter, 76, 166-167
Gates, Horatio, 23, 26, 30, 40, 44, 79, 120, 145, 153, 167, 184, 190, 193, 196, 202
Geary, James, 156
Gerard de Rayneval, Conrad Alexandre, 17, 18, 27, 30, 31, 34, 43, 46, 49, 51, 59, 65, 81-82, 83, 85, 86, 92-93, 95, 97, 104, 110, 112, 113, 128, 167, 182
Gerry, Elbridge, 17, 18-19, 34, 53, 108, 124, 148, 167-168
Gibbons, Mrs., 19
Gibson, John, 146, 147, 150, 168
Gill, Mr., 71
Gist, Mordecai, 29, 168
Gravier, Charles (Comte de Vergennes), 51, 82, 128, 167, 168
Gray, George, 168
Grayson, William, 31, 168
Greene, Nathaniel, 33, 41, 74, 76-77, 80, 107-108, 148, 110, 160, 169, 188
Grey, Mr., 99
Griffin, Cyrus, 46, 150, 151, 169
Griffin, Samuel, 169

Hamilton, James, 39, 169
Hamilton, Gov., 202
Harnett, Cornelius, 150, 169-170
Harrison, Col., 87
Hart, John, 49, 170
Hartley, Thomas, 45, 170
Harvie, John, 39, 170-171
Hawthorn, Col., 118

Index

Heath, William, 79, 171
Hele, Christopher, 30, 45, 56, 68, 79, 171
Henry, Patrick, 6, 60, 94, 104, 171, 179
Henry, William, 111
Hewes, Joseph, 147, 171-172
Hill; Whitmel, 36, 49, 172
Hogun, James, 29, 172
Holker, John, 53, 110, 118, 121, 172
Hollingsworth, ———, 89
Holten, Samuel, 37, 128, 135, 172-173
Honsecker, Col., 94
Hooper, Robert Lettice, 36, 173
Hopkinson, Francis, 24, 173
Horton, Azariah, 67, 69, 102
Houston, William Churchill, 9, 111, 118, 119, 128, 141, 173
Houston, John, 42, 90-91, 173-174
Howe, Robert, 38, 60, 174
Howe, Sir William, 159, 166
Howell, Joseph, 79-80, 174
Huger, Col., 29
Huntington, Jabez, 174
Huntington, Samuel, 113, 122, 128, 129, 133, 146, 174

Indiana claims, 130-131, 137-138, 144, 185, 198
Irish rebellion, 124-125
Irvine, William, 174-175
Irwin, Gen., 74
Izard, Ralph, 78, 93, 99-100, 175

Jackson, P., 43
Jay, John, 14, 15, 18, 28, 57, 70, 73, 107, 113, 120, 131, 132-133, 135, 139, 150, 158, 175, 180

Jefferson, Thomas, 6, 159, 162, 171, 179, 202
Jenifer, ———, 104
Jennings, Edmund, 134, 176
John Fell & Co., 7
Johnson, Joshua, 134
Johnson, Philip, 43
Johnson, Thomas, 89-90, 176

Kennedy, Samuel, 176
Kennedy, Sarah, 44, 47, 176
Knobelauch, Baron de, 123-124, 176

Labouchere, ———, 134
Lafayette, Marquis de (Marie Joseph Paul Yves Roche Gilbert du Motier), 24, 42, 166, 176-177, 183
Longworthy, Edward, 34, 177
Laurens, Henry, 15, 17, 18, 19, 20, 21, 28, 29, 33, 34, 36, 40, 44, 52, 53, 64, 74, 75, 88, 90-91, 102, 104, 112, 125-126, 132, 134, 141, 143, 144, 150, 177, 186
Laurens, John, 20, 134, 177-178, 179
Laurens-Morris affair, 10, 29-30, 33, 43-44, 44-45, 186
Lee, Arthur, 15, 34, 47, 50, 78, 79, 81-83, 94, 96, 100, 114, 123, 125, 126, 127, 131-132, 155, 161, 166, 175, 176, 177, 178, 179, 187, 194
Lee, Charles, 18, 20, 52, 178-179
Lee, Francis Lightfoot, 179
Lee, Richard Henry, 36, 51, 53, 56, 64, 65, 75, 82-83, 179
Lee, William, 50, 78, 99-100, 125, 179

Leonidas, 108
Levy, Mr., 16
Lewis, Francis, 18, 19, 72, 110, 180
Lincoln, Benjamin, 34, 36, 37, 38, 57, 70, 71, 73, 91, 110, 146, 180, 189, 190
Livingston, Henry Brockholst, 139-140, 180
Livingston, William, 13, 86, 130, 180
Lopez, Aaron, 44, 181
Lovell, James, 63, 75, 103, 181
Lowndes, Rawlins, 38, 42, 181
Loziers, ———, 22, 157, 181
Luzerne, Anne Caesar de la, 145-146, 148, 167, 182

McComb, John, 119, 182
McDowell, James, 31
McIntosh, Lachlan, 6, 34, 40, 67, 157, 182
McKean, Thomas, 20, 21, 34, 76, 82-83, 103, 108, 117, 123, 128, 182, 197
McNeil, Hector, 32, 49, 183
McNutt, Alexander, 70, 183
McPherson, William, 29, 69, 183
Madison, James, 159
Malbone, Col., 115
Marchant, Henry, 112, 183
Marrinor, Mr., 13
Marschalk, Susanna, 6
Mason, David, 44, 45, 183
Mathews, ———, 93, 128
Maxwell, William, 21, 53, 58, 91, 184
Meade, Maj., 71-72
Meason, George, 111
Mercier, ———, 119, 135
Mifflin, Thomas, 52, 184
Milligan, James, 146, 147, 150
Mitchell, ———, 53-54
Montfort, Julius de, 35, 184

Morgan, Daniel, 91, 184
Morgan, George, 130-131, 137-138, 144, 182, 184-185, 198
Morgan, John, 101, 185
Morris, Gouverneur, 17, 21, 25, 47, 53-54, 60, 62, 76, 105, 185
Morris, Robert, (Chief Justice of N.J.), 25, 185-186
Morris, Robert, (financier), 29, 33, 43-44, 46, 172, 177, 186
Moses, Isaac, 14, 73
Moskhk, Susanna, 6
Moultrie, William, 110, 186
Muhlenberg, John Peter Gabriel, 76, 186
Mumford, Thomas, 21, 22, 187

Negroes, 52, 62, 64-65, 68
Neilson, John, 13, 187
Nelson, Thomas, 51, 56, 187
Nevers, ———, 70
New York Gazetteer, 192
Noarth, ———, 67
Nova Scotia, 57, 70

Paca, William, 33, 34, 37, 40, 52, 56, 64, 67, 81-82, 103, 104, 105, 128, 135, 187
Paine, Thomas, 25, 27-28, 29, 32-33, 65, 68-69, 75, 76, 96, 186, 187-188
Parker, James, 8
Passern, Lewis D., 49
Peabody, Nathaniel, 123, 135, 188
Penet, Peter, 41, 188
Pennsylvania-Benedict Arnold dispute, 40, 46-47, 51, 53-54, 62-63, 68-69, 80

Index

Pennsylvania Magazine, or *American Monthly Museum,* 153
The Pennsylvania Packet, or the *General Advertiser,* 163
Penny, Timothy, 49
Peterboro, 7
Petersfield, 7, 13, 125
Pettit, Charles, 103, 108, 110, 160, 188
Phillips, William, 23, 30, 35-36, 94, 147-148, 188-189
Pinckney, Thomas, 70, 189
Plater, George, 56, 82-83, 189
Potter, James, 94, 189
Potts, Jonathan, 72-73, 189-190
Powell, Jeremiah, 44, 47-48, 49
Prescott, William, 33, 190
Prevost, Augustine, 70, 190
Pulaski, Casmir, 16, 41, 42, 45, 48, 184, 190
Putnam, Israel, 28, 58, 190-191, 195

Rawlings, Moses, 35, 191
Read, Thomas, 191
Reed, Joseph, 37, 40, 44, 48-49, 51, 53, 67, 72, 80, 82, 191
Richards, ———, 157, 181
Riedesel, Baron Friedrich Adolph, 148, 191-192
Rivington, James, 90, 192
Roach, Patrick, 51
Roberdeau, Daniel, 24, 36, 192
Robertson, General, 8
Rochambeau, 165
Rogers, ———, 70
Root, Jesse, 19, 21, 24, 36, 37, 64, 192
Ross, John, 47, 192
Rush, Benjamin, 155, 189
Rutgers, Henry, 66, 69, 192-193
Rutherford, Walter, 8

Rutledge, John, 60, 110, 193
St. Clair, Arthur, 17, 193
Schuyler, Philip John, 7, 25, 26, 31, 59, 68, 74, 85, 167, 193-194, 200
Scudder, Nathaniel, 9, 16, 29, 79, 83, 92, 94, 100, 102, 104, 105, 109, 110, 111, 123, 130, 131, 141, 194
Searle, James, 8, 19, 29, 34, 51, 60, 88, 110, 133, 194
Sherman, Roger, 105, 113, 194
Shippen, William, 43, 195
Slaves, 52, 64-65, 191
Smith, James, 17, 19, 24, 33, 195
Smith, Johnston, 36, 37
Smith, Jonathan Bayard, 18, 21, 30, 195
Smith, Meriwether, 34, 47, 54, 62, 63, 64-65, 66, 88, 90, 92-93, 104, 128
Sons of Liberty, 192
Spencer, Joseph, 94, 102, 195-196
Steuben, Friedrich Wilhelm Ludolf Gerhard Augustin (Baron von Steuben), 47-48, 70, 196
Stevenson, James, 111
Steward, ———, 82
Stirling, Sir Thomas, 196
Sterling, William, Earl of, 30, 196
Sullivan, John, 25, 27, 33, 135, 147-148, 151, 184, 196-197
Summer, Jethro, 29, 197
Sutton, John, 19

Temple, John, 14, 15, 197
Thompson, William, 20, 21, 94, 197
Thompson, John H., 9

211

Delegate from New Jersey.

Thomson, Charles, 125, 197-198
Thull, ———, 134
Trent, William, 130, 137-138, 144, 198
Trumbull, John, 133, 198
Trumbull, Jonathan, 46, 56, 65, 67, 198-199
Trumbull, Jonathan (Jr.), 133, 146, 199
Trumbull, Joseph, 65-66, 69, 84, 199

Van Courtland, Philip, 76, 199
Van Schaick, Goose, 86-87, 200
Van Zandt, Wynant, 8
Vandalia, 130-131, 138, 144, 198
Varick, Richard, 43, 200
Varley, Felix, 49-50
Vergennes, Comte de, *see* Gravier, Charles
Vermont: question of statehood, 95, 97-98, 103, 128, 153, 185
Von Steuben, Baron, *see* Steuben

Wadsworth, Jeremiah, 35-36, 99, 187, 200
Ward, Israil, 24
Ward, Stephen, 24, 47
Waring, ———, 151
Washington, George, 16, 17, 18, 20, 22, 23, 24, 25, 27, 28, 30, 31, 34, 35, 38-39, 40, 41, 53, 56, 58, 59, 66, 76, 79, 84, 86, 91, 97, 99, 102, 112, 115, 117-118, 120, 137, 143, 151, 155, 157, 165, 167, 168, 169, 171, 176, 177, 179, 181, 184, 190, 191, 193, 196, 199, 201, 202
Waterbury, David, 94, 201
Watkins, ———, 41-42
Wayne, Anthony, 20, 115, 117-118, 179, 186, 201
Weare, M., 14-15
Webb, Samuel Blatchley, 94, 147, 201
Wharton, Joseph, 133
Whipple, William, 34, 36, 76, 151, 201-202
Whitehead, ———, 14
Whiting, William, 67, 202
Wickoff, ———, 105, 106, 111
Wilkinson, James, 115, 117, 202
Willing, James, 68, 202
Witherspoon, John, 9, 16, 17, 28, 47, 49, 52, 66, 71, 72, 75, 79, 83, 92, 94, 111, 112, 139, 143, 144, 148, 202
Wood, ———, 94

Yeates, Jasper, 66-67, 203
Young, Moses, 19

Zedwitz, Herman Baron, 34, 66, 203